THE
NEEDLEPOINT WORKBOOK
OF
TRADITIONAL DESIGNS

The Needlepoint Workbook of Traditional Designs

By Cecelia Felcher

DIAGRAMS AND GRAPHS BY
JEROME FELCHER
PHOTOGRAPHS BY SALVATORE LOPES

HAWTHORN BOOKS, INC.
PUBLISHERS / *New York*

To my husband,
Jerry, whose love, patience, guidance,
and talent made ideas become reality

THE NEEDLEPOINT WORKBOOK OF TRADITIONAL DESIGNS

Copyright © 1973 by Cecelia Felcher. Copyright under International and Pan-American Copyright Conventions. All rights reserved, including the right to reproduce this book or portions thereof in any form, except for the inclusion of brief quotations in a review. All inquiries should be addressed to Hawthorn Books, Inc., 260 Madison Avenue, New York, New York 10016. This book was manufactured in the United States of America and published simultaneously in Canada by Prentice-Hall of Canada, Limited, 1870 Birchmount Road, Scarborough, Ontario.

Library of Congress Catalog Card Number: 72-7781
ISBN: Hardbound edition, 0-8015-5340-7
    Paperback edition, 0-8015-5342-3

2 3 4 5 6 7 8 9 10

Acknowledgments

Most grateful appreciation is extended to my many friends for their help and encouragement during the writing of this book.

Usually last, but first in my book, special thanks go to Minna Zaret for her quick mind and nimble fingers.

Special thanks too, to: Elizabeth Malament, who never said no; Harry Freed, for his technical know-how in photography; my son, Robert, who helped with the typing; the women who worked to make the beautiful pillows for the book—Gladys Blum, Myra Fox, Maxine Rudman, Helen Tandler, Theresia Visser, Charlene Waldman, and Shari Wolfson; M. and Z. Decorators, of Bayside, who upholstered pillows on short notice.

Contents

Introduction

The idea for this book came after years of doing a variety of needlepoint on trips to Norway, Denmark, France, and England. Each time I finished a piece, I felt a sense of well-being. I enjoyed the work and had created something beautiful and useful; a pillow, a footstool cover, a belt, or a chair seat. Yet somehow I was not completely satisfied. The designs were not mine, and often even the colors were prescribed for me. I attempted to design my own canvases with waterproof paints, but I soon learned something I had always suspected —I was not an artist. My flowers, animals, and figures were too primitive and were not acceptable to me, even after many painstaking hours of work.

An unfortunate event occurred which provided me with unexpected time to solve my dilemma. My husband's illness made it necessary to take a leave of absence from my teaching position in a Long Island high school. During his long convalescence an idea occurred to me that designers discovered many years ago. They borrowed from the past! They adapted ancient traditional designs to their own needs, arranging them in their own creative manners, which resulted in something bearing the mark of their personalities. My love of antique Oriental rugs led me to search through our own collection of old rugs and beautifully illustrated rug books. What fertile fields!

Oriental handmade rugs have been popular with collectors since medieval times and perhaps even earlier. Western civilization has always been in awe of the unique quality of each work of art. A careful study of carpets from Turkey, Persia, Caucasus, and China reveals the creator's own expression or individuality. Additions to basic themes, differences in the number and arrangement of traditional borders, and a slight change in dimension make each piece of work a new experience.

The rugs were considered an aid for meditation and inspiration. They were, for some Orientals, their only piece of "furniture" and were used as sofas, cushions, welcome mats, and for prayer. For some illiterate Nomadic tribes the carpets were a form of writing "anonymous poems of a community more moving than the verses of their greatest poets," says Gans-Ruedin in the introduction to his book *Oriental Carpets*.

After much searching I decided to make a small rug composed of four borders and three center triangles, all geometrically planned. One does not have to be an artist to translate a geometric design to graph paper. My first attempts were sloppy, but with the help of my very cooperative husband I managed to get those first designs down on graph paper successfully. I found it simple to follow the graph, since many of the elements were repeated several times. The precision of the designs together with the rich colors of the Persian yarns created a spectacular response. People observing me working at meetings, beauty parlors, or on vacations admired and questioned me about this unusual needlepoint. My unmarked canvas, with no visible graph, aroused much interest. (I usually save the repeat borders or the background for working publicly and the complicated centers for the quiet of my home.) I encouraged my friends to undertake these fascinating designs. It was then that I decided to seek designs from other cultures to adapt for needlepoint and to share these ideas and designs with all needlepointers who, like me, have become bored with store-bought, painted canvases and want to experience the thrill of doing needlepoint rich in tradition yet uniquely their own.

I know you will enjoy selecting your own border and center arrangements, changing colors, proportions, and even adding your own adaptations to the ones found in this workbook. Don't be afraid to experiment, and above all don't be a color-coward.

Have fun and good luck.

Author's Note

Needlepoint is probably the least complicated of all the needlecrafts, yet it holds endless fascination in its unlimited potential for variation. It is a soothing antidote for a hectic world, a healthful replacement for the harmful tobacco weed, and a sedate activity when rest is required.

The novice will find here all the necessary instructions to embark on an exciting new hobby or possibly even a new way of life. For the experienced needlepointer this workbook should lead to unlimited creative experiences.

PART I.

Before You Start to Work

Materials

Needlepoint is embroidery or hand-stitching on canvas, usually done in wool, occasionally in silk or cotton. The stitches of basic needlepoint all slant in one direction.

1. CANVAS

There are essentially two types of canvas used for needlepoint: the mono, or single-thread mesh, and the penelope, or double-thread mesh. Either can be used satisfactorily. The single-thread mesh is less confusing for the beginner, since there is only one possible hole for the needle to enter. The penelope holds its shape better and can also be used for making small (petit point) stitches. In either case the canvas is readily available and may be purchased by the yard in most needlecraft stores. It comes in varying widths (36", 40", 54") and anywhere from 3- to 20-to-the-inch mesh. (Each mesh will eventually become a stitch.) Remember, the more threads to the inch, the smaller your stitches will be. *Caution:* When you buy canvas, make sure it is cotton and not a synthetic, which will be stiff and difficult to work with. Avoid a canvas that has knots or uneven rows. Don't be shy about refusing to accept an irregular piece of canvas.

Mono canvas

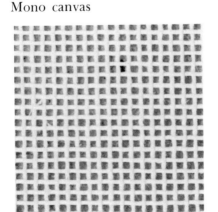

Penelope canvas

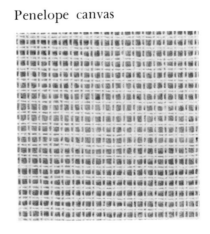

2. THREAD

The most popular thread used for needlepoint is a three-strand Persian wool yarn. I prefer this yarn, as it is available in an endless assortment of beautiful colors delicately shaded in color families. It is easily separated if only one or two strands are needed. This yarn may be purchased by the piece, ounce, or pound. Naturally, if you are making a large item, it will be less expensive to buy the wool by the pound. I hesitate to quote any prices, as they frequently change. Persian yarn has a very tight twist, making a durable finish for rugs, footstools, and seat covers. English and French tapestry and crewel yarns are also used for needlepoint. They do not separate as easily as the Persian yarn if a lighter weight is called for but are certainly satisfactory and also are available in a wide range of colors. The English yarns have a range of muted shades that are unequaled in their subtlety. *Caution:* Knitting yarns are not as tightly twisted as Persian, crewel, or tapestry yarns and will not hold up as well during the work or after. Remember, the yarn is abused by the constant pulling in and out of the canvas and therefore must be strong to begin with. Don't look for bargains. The amount of labor involved warrants the slightly higher cost of the best materials. Always use pure wool!

3. NEEDLES

All canvas work needles are made of steel, are blunt, and have long eyes. (No problems with threading or pricking.) The size of the needle used is determined by the thickness of the yarn and the size of the mesh. The smallest needles, for petit point, are numbered in the 20's. As the size of the needle increases, the number decreases. For a gros-point canvas of 10 mesh to the inch I use a #18 needle.

When you decide what size mesh you will use and the thickness of the thread, you will easily determine the proper size by trying to thread the needle. If you have trouble pulling the thread through the eye, a larger needle is called for. A heavy needle used on a small mesh will push the threads out of shape. The cost of the needles is negligible, so I keep extras around and at least one extra always in my current work. I learned to do this after an unhappy experience with a lost needle. Once, at the beginning of an overseas flight, my needle slipped out of my hand, and no amount of searching revealed the small elusive piece of steel. The remainder of the flight was spent in mulling over how much I could have accomplished and vowing always to carry an extra needle.

4. SCISSORS

Treat yourself to a fine pair of small pointed scissors; you won't regret the initial expense. Nothing is more frustrating than a pair of dull scissors. The pointed end will be useful if you have to rip out stitches, and we all do at times. Scissors are easily lost or misplaced even when you are sitting quietly at your work. I never was able to remember where I had put them last—on the table nearby, on my lap, back in the yarn bag, or perhaps they slipped into the side of the chair. To avoid a frantic search each time I need to cut a thread, I now tie a long piece of yarn through the scissor loop, knot it, and wear it around my neck while I work. I suggest using a thread of a bright color not being used for your current work, thus making it simple to identify and remove from your bag. A cork is good protection for the sharp points of your scissors when they are not in use.

5. THIMBLE

A thimble will protect your finger when you push the needle through the canvas. Most people cannot work without one. Buy a good quality thimble; a poorly made one has a rough finish and will fray the wool.

6. MASKING TAPE

The simplest way to keep canvas from raveling is to fold masking tape over the raw edges before you start to work. This not only protects the canvas but keeps the edge from catching and scratching. Use tape that is at least one inch in width.

7. GRAPH PAPER

You might want to lay out your own design on paper. To get the exact size of your finished work, you must use graph paper ruled to the same size as your canvas mesh. For example, if you are using #10 mesh, then use 10-to-the-inch ruled graph paper. If you are working out a small section of a repeat pattern and don't feel it necessary to see a true size, then use large graph rulings so it will be easier to work from. Try 4- or 5-to-the-inch ruled graph paper for these repeat patterns; it will simplify things. You should not find it necessary to re-work any of the designs in this workbook; they are all done for you. Later, on page 15 I tell you how to figure the size of a finished canvas.

Stitches

There are many stitch variations used in needlepoint. For all of the designs in this book you need only learn two simple stitches: the continental (tent stitch) and the basket weave. Both stitches have the same appearance on the right side, a slanting half cross stitch, but the backs are quite different.

Continental stitch (front)

Continental stitch (back)

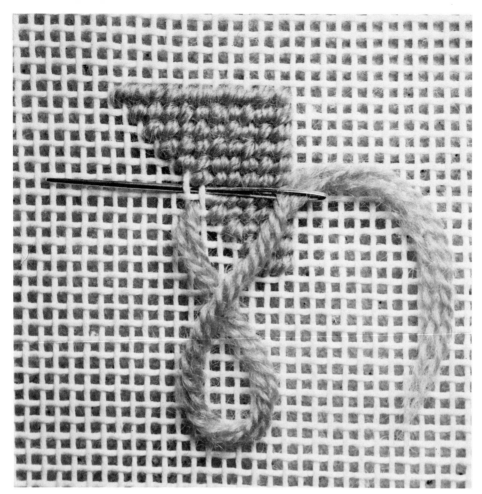

Basket-weave stitch (front)

Basket-weave stitch (back)

The size of the canvas mesh determines whether the stitch is a petit point (tiny) or gros point (large).

1. CONTINENTAL

The continental stitch, sometimes called the tent stitch, is the stitch most generally used for needlepoint work. It is quick, easy to perform, and the slanting stitches formed on the wrong side provide extra strength to the work. The one disadvantage inherent in the continental stitch is that it tends to pull the canvas out of shape. This can generally be corrected when the canvas is blocked. The stitch is worked in the following manner:

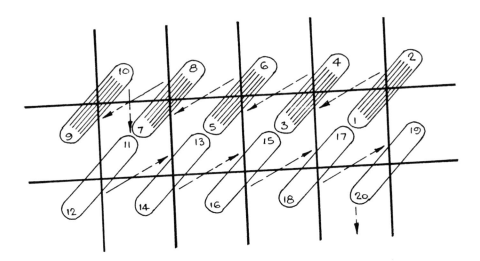

Work is started at the top right-hand corner of the design. For the first stitch, bring the needle up at 1 and down at 2. For the second stitch, bring the needle up at 3 and down at 4, and for the third stitch, bring the needle up at 5 and down at 6. Just keep repeating along the row. All odd numbers are up from back to front. All even numbers are down from front to back. For the second row turn the canvas around and continue in the opposite direction. With a little practice you should have no problem with this stitch.

2. BASKET WEAVE

The basket weave stitch is wonderful for filling in background. It is fascinating to do, keeps the canvas in shape (unlike the continental stitch), and forms a sturdy finish for a

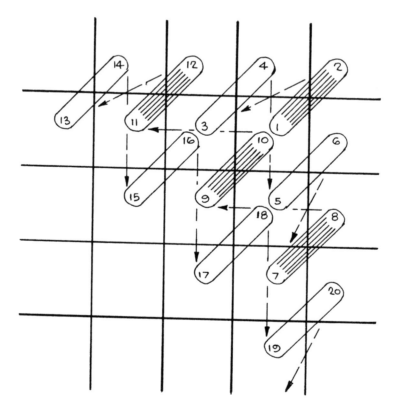

piece of needlepoint that may be subjected to heavy wear. I try to use it as often as possible even though it requires one-third more yarn than the continental stitch. The wrong side looks so lovely, truly like a basket weave, that I've been tempted to work it in reverse—with the wrong side becoming the finished side. You might try it just for fun.

Caution: Always go up one row and down another when doing the basket-weave stitch. Two rows done in the same direction will cause a slight ridge that can be very noticeable in a large background area. Before you attempt any design, practice both stitches until you feel completely confident and relaxed using them. It is the evenness you acquire with assurance that makes for a smoothly finished piece.

Caution: Don't pull or tug as you work, but use a smooth, rhythmic movement, *placing* rather than *sewing* stitches on the canvas. The tension should be even and the stitches loose. Test by slipping the needle between the finished stitch and the canvas. The needle should slide under with no difficulty.

The odd numbers, 1, 3, 5, 7, etc., indicate that the needle comes up from back to front. The even numbers, 2, 4, 6, 8, etc., indicate that the needle goes down from front to back.

Keep in mind that all diagonal movements of the needle are on top, on the finished surface, and that all horizontal and vertical movements of the needle are on the underside, or backside of the canvas, except for the first stitch of a new row.

For the first stitch, bring the needle up at 1 and down at 2. For the second stitch, bring the needle up at 3 and down at 4, and for the third stitch, bring the needle up at 5 and down at 6, and keep on going up one row and down the other until you have filled in the area.

Always start from top right-hand corner of the canvas. If you are left-handed start from the bottom left-hand corner and work diagonally up toward the right-hand side of the canvas.

Decisions, Decisions!

For a new recruit to needlepointing I usually suggest making a pillow. It is easy to handle—not too large nor too small—and becomes a practical source of joy for all to admire.

A good size mesh for overall use is the #10 mono. It is large enough to be worked quickly yet not so large that it will appear indelicate. Use a #18 needle and three-strand Persian yarn. If you use penelope canvas, which, as I have said before, will hold the stitches in shape better, you will probably be able to use two strands (rather than the full three) of Persian. Tapestry yarn may be used as it comes out of the skein. Always do a few practice stitches with the wool you plan to use. If it does not cover the canvas, it is too thin. If it is too thick to pull through, use a thinner yarn. Before long you will have no trouble judging the proper yarn thickness for the canvas you are using.

Decide on the approximate size of your finished pillow. The average size is about 12 by 14 inches. However, any size you choose will lend itself nicely to the traditional designs in this workbook.

Cut your canvas about one inch larger than the finished size on all sides. That is, for a finished pillow measuring 12 by 14, cut the canvas to measure 14 by 16, and cover the raw edges with masking tape.

Your canvas is now ready to be worked. What to put on it is the big decision!

Browse through the designs; choose some that please you. Select several borders and one main center pattern. Count the number of stitches in the width of each border and add them together. Remember that you will have 10 stitches to the inch if you are using 10-mesh canvas. On a 12- by 14-inch pillow you will have 120 stitches on the sides and 140 stitches in the width. Now, if the borders you have selected add up to 35 stitches in width, then subtract 35 stitches from each of the four sides, leaving a center field measuring 50 by 70 stitches. Select one large center as illustrated on page 222 or a small scatter design that you can repeat several times, as illustrated on page 217. Decide how you would like the borders arranged. I like to have a narrow one on each side of a wide one, but it is a personal choice. It is more satisfying to create your own scheme.

If you are unsure of how your choice will work out, you might try to copy onto graph paper about two inches of each border you have selected. Then, cut them apart and try them in various positions until you are pleased with the arrangement. If you want to get an idea of the finished effect in color, you could use crayons to fill in the graph. Somehow I don't think you can go far wrong. All of these traditional designs mix well and will look spectacular on your finished work. You might decide to use just borders going around the canvas with no center design, as illustrated in Plate 21, or you could make bands of borders, as illustrated on page 223. Here is where your own individuality will shine through. Remember that the smaller the canvas mesh, the more designs you will need to cover your area.

2. COLORS

Since color selection is so personal, I do not like to recommend specific colors. I do suggest however that certain designs are best outlined in dark colors, such as black, dark brown, or navy. In some designs areas of light colors are effective. Here, white, beige, or the palest tone of a particular color may be used most successfully. Other areas look best when done in medium tones. Your own taste and requirements should guide your selection of colors. If you know where your finished article will be used, try to use colors that look best in that room or on a particular sofa or chair. Belts usually look best with solid-color dresses, so don't be afraid to use color freely on your belt.

I usually experiment with a handful of the colors I am considering for my next piece of needlepoint. Most yarn shops will give you the opportunity to browse at length and match a few strands of each color before you make a final decision.

COLOR KEY

☐ Palest color (white, beige, pale yellow, etc.)

⊡ Light middle color (tan, gold, light blue, etc.)

⊙ Middle color (blue, green, red, yellow, etc.)

⊠ Dark middle color (dark tones of any of the above)

▨ Background color

■ Black, brown, or navy blue

3. QUANTITY OF YARN

The yarn required to cover one square inch of #10 canvas averages about 1¼ yards if you are using the continental stitch. For the basket-weave stitch, figure about 1¾ yards per square inch. Of course quantities vary with the individual's work habits and the pattern. If your tension is loose, you will require more yarn than someone who works tightly. If the pattern calls for frequent color changes, you will use more yarn than you would for a two-color pattern.

Roughly, figure an average of 1½ yards per square inch, assuming that you will use some basket-weave and some continental stitches. To find out the total number of square inches in your piece, multiply the width by the length. When you purchase your yarn, try to gauge the proportions of each color your design will use. When you are all finished with your computations, buy some extra of each color, and you should be safe. It is very frustrating to run out of a color in the middle of your work. I try to buy yarn from a shop that is pleasant about exchanging leftovers. If you check before making your purchase, you will surely find a shop willing to cooperate with you. I must admit that I have an antique wooden tool box filled with odds and ends of every conceivable color. They come in handy when I need a bit of color here and there.

PART II.

Beginning to Work

Preparation

You are now prepared to begin work. The canvas is cut and taped, your designs and arrangement are decided upon, the wool is selected and purchased, the scissors are hanging around your neck on a long thread (not one of the colors you will be using), and your extra needles are in the sewing bag.

1. DEFINING OUTER LIMITS

I begin most work by defining the outer limits. I do one row all around the canvas, generally in a color that will be used for my backing. When you are using a design that has a one-stitch center or any odd number of stitches, use an odd number of stitches in your outline row. If your center design has an even number of stitches, start with an even number. If you should change your mind in midstream, don't worry. You can only be one stitch off center, and no one but you will know the difference. After you have outlined your canvas, thread a needle with black or red sewing thread and make a running stitch across the center, top to bottom, and side to side. Leave a four- or five-inch piece of thread loose at the edges so you will have no trouble pulling it out when you are finished. This running stitch will be the center guide for all your work.

2. THREADING THE NEEDLE

Thread your tapestry needle by folding about an inch of yarn over the needle, pinching it firmly, and sliding it off the needle between your thumb and index finger. Then push the eye of the needle over the fold as you slowly release your fingers. Pull the yarn through the eye until the needle is about one third of the way down. After you do this a few times, it will come to you with ease.

The length of your thread is important. Never use a piece longer than 18 inches. The longer the thread, the weaker the last few inches will be. Each time you pull the thread through the canvas, the yarn loses body, thereby causing the thread to thin out and weaken. This thin thread is easily noticeable on your work, especially when filling in background. You may think it saves time to use a longer thread; in reality it takes more time to pull each stitch through because of the greater length.

3. BEGINNING AND ENDING THREADS

Starting to work on a blank canvas presents a problem. To what do you anchor the first thread? Knots are never used on needlepoint. The simplest solution is to leave about an inch and a half of thread hanging loosely on the underside of the first stitch. You will return to it later. Continue working the first thread, and when you are ready to end it, weave the needle in and out through 8 or 10 stitches on the underside. Clip thread very close to the canvas so that the loose ends will not interfere with later work. Now go back to the loose thread of the first stitch, thread the needle and weave the end under the first 8 to 10 stitches. Clip close to canvas. Start each new thread by weaving under stitches of the same color wherever possible, ending where your next stitch will begin.

If you are using two-strand yarn for a particular piece of work, there is a very simple way to start each thread without weaving under stitches. Using a single strand, double it and thread the two loose ends through the needle. Now come up through the canvas to the right side just as you would for any stitch, but leave about one inch of the looped end on the underside of the canvas. Now go down as you normally would, pulling the needle through the loop. Pull gently, and you now have an anchor that will never pull out. Really simple.

Stitching

1. STARTING BORDERS

Most patterns calling for borders and a center are best started at the outer edge and worked toward the center. This will make it simpler to center your main design or place repeat scatter designs on the center field.

Always start at the center of each side (your sewing thread will be your guide), and work out toward each corner from both sides. Do not go to the very end of the row. Stop at the completion of a pattern when there is not enough room for another complete repeat. Then work from the center out on remaining sides. Unless you are working with a square canvas, the design on the horizontal side will not end at the same place as the design on the vertical side. Don't be concerned. Your four corners do not have to be the same. Corners may be treated in many ways. (See illustrations of finished articles for ideas.) Try to be original; it is your creation. Don't be meek about experimenting. Sometimes the simplest solution is the best. A single row of a contrasting color between borders is effective and helps to define each new border.

Single Patterns

When you have completed all your borders and want to use one single center design, work it from the middle of the design out. Your sewing thread will mark the point at which you begin. When you have completed the center, fill in the remaining canvas with your background color using the basket-weave stitch. If you think there is too much background between the borders and center design, it is not too late to add another border.

Repeated Scatters

If you want to repeat a scatter design, count the number of stitches in the width and length of the center field. Count the number of stitches in the scatter design. Figure out by simple division how many you can fit into the center field. Do not squeeze too many into the space. It is better to leave more space between designs.

When all work is completed, pull out the sewing-thread guide.

3. ADAPTING BORDERS AND CENTERS FOR SPECIFIC ITEMS

Small Items

For items other than pillows use the same general directions adapting the number of repeated borders to the size of the article being made. Most belts will require only one or two borders at most. Eyeglass cases might have one small scatter or several narrow borders.

Rugs

If you are ambitious, patient, and tired of doing small projects, you would probably enjoy doing a rug. If you think of it as just an oversized pillow, it won't seem frightening. I hesitate to suggest doing a rug in squares, as putting it together presents many problems. If you are prepared to have the finishing done professionally (it will be very costly), by all means do the squares. They are certainly easier to carry around and offer opportunity for unique designs. On the other hand, a 3- by 5-foot scatter rug can be carried with you. The canvas will seem stiff at first but will soften with use and will roll easily. Finishing a one-piece rug will be much less costly than squares. Realistically, anything larger than 3 by 5 will be cumbersome and tiresome unless you are an unusually strong needlepointer.

Since you will be repeating your border patterns over and over on a rug, make absolutely certain that you are happy with your design and color selections. When you have made your decision about the borders, do a small practice section of each in the arrangement and colors you have chosen. This sample should help you make your final decision.

The #10 canvas, 40 inches wide, is my choice for a needlepoint rug. Smaller size mesh will make the task seem endless. Larger mesh will not be as long-lasting nor as delicate but is certainly worth doing. Again the choice is yours. For the #10 canvas use the full three-strand Persian yarn.

Selecting your overall scheme will take careful calculations. Most center and scatter designs can be enlarged without losing character by simply doubling or tripling or quadrupling each stitch shown on the graph. For example, where a pattern shows 5 stitches, you might want to do 10, 15, or 20 stitches. You must, however, increase consistently throughout each design. Remember that on #10 canvas you have 10 stitches to the inch. This makes your arithmetic simple. If you enlarge center or scatter designs you do not necessarily have to enlarge the border designs.

Unlike pillows, rugs are best started with the center design. One, two, three, or even four center designs, depending on the size of the canvas, may be used. If your overall scheme calls for repeating a scatter design, do these first also.

After you have completed your center, start the outermost

PART III.

Finishing

Blocking

Most canvases will need blocking or reshaping by the time you have finished all your needlepoint stitching. Blocking is not always an easy job, as the canvas may be terribly distorted. I usually recommend that the blocking and finishing be done professionally. A piece of needlepoint in which you have invested much time, energy, and love deserves a professional finisher. These days most upholsterers and art shops are experienced at handling needlepoint and will do justice to your work.

If you should decide to do the finishing yourself, you will need a few pieces of equipment: a large board, plywood, or a drawing board that is several inches larger than your canvas; a draftsman's T square; a large plastic triangle with a 90-degree corner; rustproof pushpins (I prefer pushpins to thumbtacks, as they are easier to remove), a towel, and a sponge.

Place the towel on the board, and put the canvas face down on the towel. With a wet sponge thoroughly moisten the canvas. Do not be afraid to use water; since you have used no ink or paint on your canvas, nothing will run. Pin the top edge of the work parallel to the top edge of the board. Pull the bottom into shape, making sure that the corners form right angles. Check by using the T square or a large plastic triangle, and make sure that your canvas is evenly taut. Pin all around the canvas at approximately one-inch intervals. Allow two or three days for complete drying. Keep the board in a horizontal position and avoid artificial heat during the drying process.

When you remove the canvas from the board, you might want to steam it briefly to restore the natural fluff. Hold the steam iron over the right side, making sure that you do not touch the yarn with the iron. The steam will do the work.

Backing

1. PILLOWS

The backing of a pillow should match your background color or any predominant color in your canvas. Cotton velvet is a good choice, as it comes in a wide range of colors, making it easy to find a good match. Baste the fabric to the canvas, right sides facing each other on three sides, leaving an extra two inches of fabric on the fourth side. Get as close to the last row of needlepoint stitching as possible. Machine stitch, turn inside out, and fill with a muslin pillow or just stuff with dacron (or a filling of your choice). The loose flap of the fourth side is tucked in and carefully hand stitched. If you are an experienced seamstress, welting or braiding made from your own yarn adds the professional touch when it is sewn in between the canvas and backing.

2. BELTS

Belts are not difficult to finish even for the amateur. Use grosgrain ribbon (or velvet) of the exact width of the belt for the backing. As the ribbon comes in standard widths, decide on the width you want before you select a pattern. You can always add a row or two on each side to meet the width of the ribbon. If you match the ribbon color to the color of the end rows of your design, your sewing stitches will be less noticeable.

After the belt is blocked, remove tape, trim canvas, baste the edges under the last row of needlepoint, leaving long sewing threads at each end, then press. Hemstitch the ribbon to the belt, making sure that the edges meet exactly. Pull out the basting stitches. Steam the face of the needlepoint. Attach the buckle. Try to find a buckle that the belt will slide through rather than one with sharp teeth that will fray your needlework. I like to use antique buckles, which I collect avidly. (See belts in Plate 16.)

3. FOOTSTOOLS, PIANO BENCHES, AND CHAIR SEATS

If the top of a footstool, bench, or chair slips out of its frame, it is easy to cover with needlepoint. If the tops are tacked over the side of the frame, I recommend that you have an upholsterer do the work.

For the slip-top use a filling (dacron or cotton batting) of any thickness you desire over the board, which is part of the furniture. Hold the filling in place by covering with muslin and taping to underside of the board. Next, center the blocked needlepoint on the board, turn the work upside down, and tack the edges to the board, pulling the canvas as tightly as possible. Make certain that you are pulling evenly on all sides. Check the right side of the work frequently as you go along. Mitre the corners carefully, tacking each edge separately. Slip the work back into the frame, and you are finished.

Rugs require expert blocking, and again I recommend getting a professional to do the work. Your investment in time, money, and energy warrants the expense of an expert finisher. If you really are determined to finish the rug yourself, follow the instructions for blocking using another person to help you pull the rug into shape. Don't be afraid to pull; nothing will come apart. Be sure to soak the rug thoroughly, or you will have trouble pulling it into shape. Make certain that the rug is completely dry before you remove it from the blocking board.

If you intend to use your rug as a rug rather than a wall hanging, don't line it. The dirt and grit that most certainly will end up on your rug will be trapped in the lining and may cause the threads to break because of the constant friction. An unlined rug will allow the grit to fall through and end up on the floor under your rug, where it can easily be cleaned.

Finish by trimming the edges around the rug to about three-quarters of an inch. Machine sew a two- or three-inch binding to the canvas edge. Turn and baste. Press with a damp cloth. Next, blanket-stitch along the needlepoint edge using the same color wool as was used on the end rows. Next, hand hem-stitch the binding to the wrong side of the rug. Remove basting, and you have a finished rug.

You might investigate a rubberized or latex backing that can be applied to the back of the rug with a paintbrush. This should keep the rug from sliding around on the floor. A thick padding placed on the floor under the rug will also keep it in place. Needlepoint rugs are tough, so don't be afraid to walk on yours.

PART IV.

Helpful Hints and Reminders

Relax when you work; it will help you to maintain a rhythm that will result in an even tension on your stitches.

Do not use any marking pens or pencils on your canvas which are not waterproof. There is really no reason to mark the canvas at all.

Untwist the yarn frequently while you work by turning the work upside down and allowing the yarn to hang down freely until it untwists. Twisted yarn will not cover the canvas completely.

Make certain that all your stitches go in the same direction.

If you are working on a large rug, keep it rolled on your lap or on a table while you work. The weight of it hanging down will stretch the canvas out of shape.

Each time you stop working, roll the canvas with the wrong side out, thus keeping the right side clean.

Take care to come through the holes in the canvas with your needle so that you do not split the thread of the previous row.

Rip out stitches by removing the needle from the thread and pulling out stitches with the needle tip, first from the underside, then from the front side. Alternating sides as you rip will make the task go faster and be easier on the yarn. Above all, do not attempt to go back through the hole while your needle is still threaded, as you are bound to split the previous stitch.

If you have large areas to rip, use the tip of your scissors, and gently cut through the top, then the bottom, of the stitches to be removed. Be very careful not to cut the canvas. After you have cut each stitch, pull yarn out with your needle and fingertips.

When filling in the background in continental stitch, avoid working in blocks, as this will leave lines on the right side of your work. It is better to stagger the edges of your stitches.

Never end the yarn at the end of a row when doing the basket-weave stitch. You must go up one row and down the next to avoid a ridge. If you have ended at the end of a row, you might not remember which way to go next. However, if you should forget, don't despair. Turn your work over to the wrong side, and see the direction of the last row. If it slants down, you go up; if it slants up, you go down.

Do not carry yarn across large areas when you are going on to another area of the same color. Instead, weave your yarn under the stitches you pass on the way. If the distance is great, end and start again.

Do not worry about having all your corners alike. The folk craftsman was never concerned about borders fitting into the space exactly. They were adapted by adding or taking away something when necessary. It is this sense of freedom that makes each piece of folk handicraft an individual delight.

When you do a repeat border, it is not always necessary to have a consistent pattern of *color* repeat. A little variation will make your work more interesting and unique.

You are not a machine! Your work does not have to appear machine perfect.

Place, rather than sew, your stitches on the canvas.

Never crumple your canvas while you work, rather roll it up to the area you will be working on.

If you should notice a loose stitch when examining your finished piece, insert your needle under the offending stitch on the wrong side and lift gently. This will generally do the trick. If a stitch looks too tight, do the same on the right side.

Wherever possible when starting a new row next to an already completed row of stitches, try to go in the direction that will permit your needle to go down into the completed row and up in an empty space on the canvas. It makes it easier to keep from splitting the threads with your needle.

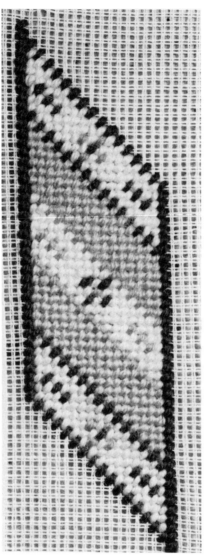

1

AFGHANISTAN BORDER

This flexible border of alternate diagonal stripes was found
on a rug from Afghanistan. It is called the barber-pole stripe.
Frequently the stripes carry small decorative patterns. It can be
made wider or narrower depending on your needs. See Plate 9
for effective use of this border.

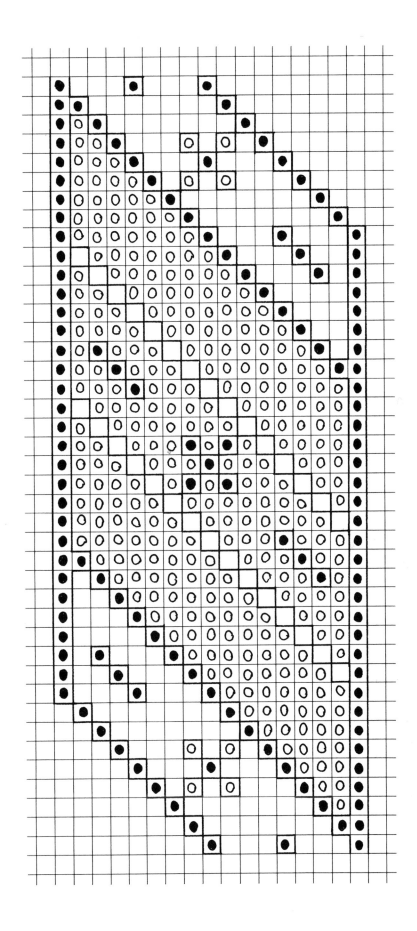

41

2

ALASKAN INDIAN BORDER

This bold design was found on a large berrying basket in the Tlingit Indian country of southeastern Alaska. The three bands are of equal width and require fifteen rows.

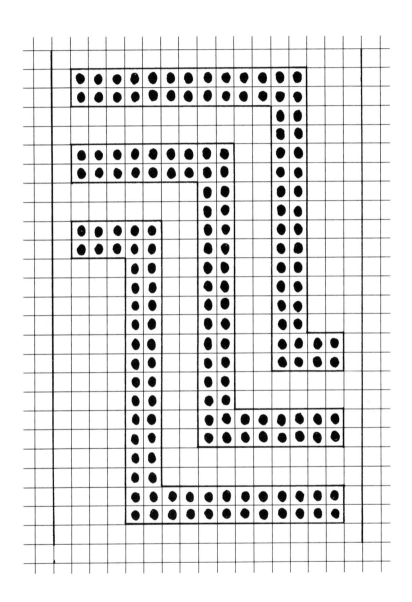

3

Alaskan Indian Border

The Tlingit Indians of Alaska call this the stick fish weir design.
Done in two colors, it requires ten rows, plus a single line on
each side.

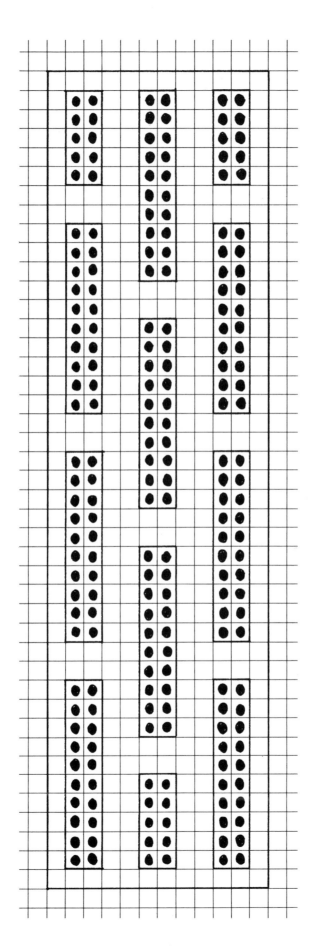

4

ALASKAN INDIAN BORDER

This is the popular "wave" pattern of the Alaskan Tlingit
Indians. It is usually done in two colors. There are nine rows plus
an outer border on each side.

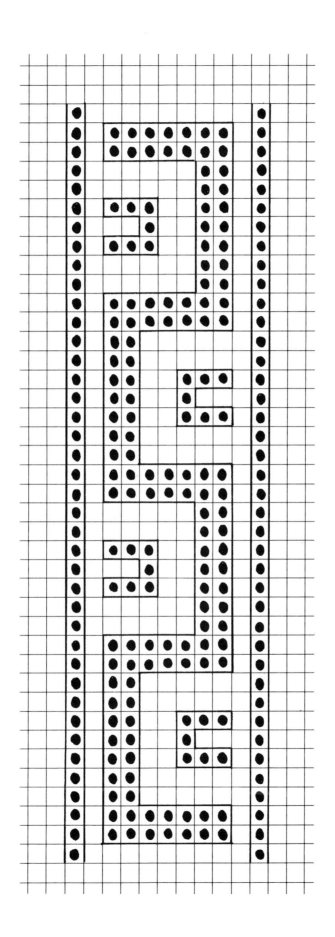

47

5

ALASKAN INDIAN BORDER

Called checkerboard design by the Alaskan Indians, this border is
found on spruce-root baskets. It is usually worked in one color
on a pale background and is fourteen rows wide with a single
border on each side.

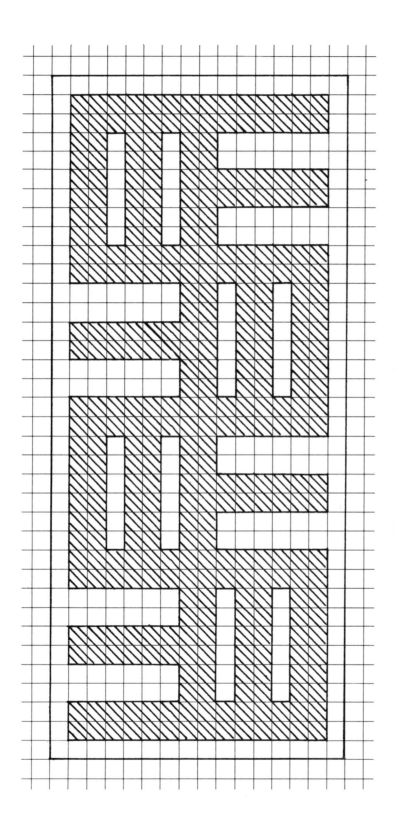

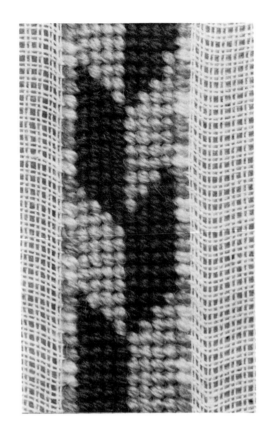

6

ALASKAN INDIAN BORDER

This Alaskan Indian border was used on woven baskets. Use
alternating colors. Notice that the line bordering the pattern is a
two-color line.

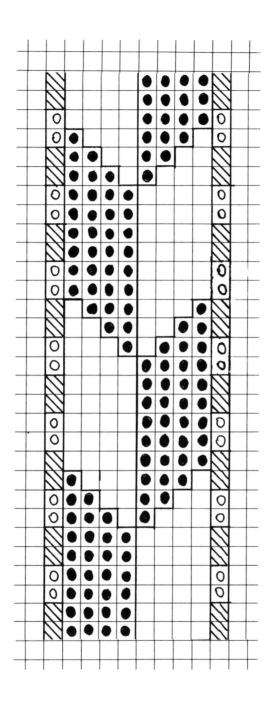

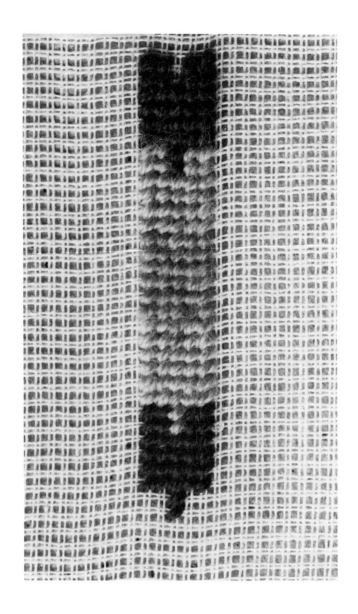

7

CAUCASIAN BORDER

Oriental border found on antique Caucasian rug. It is shown
here in three alternating colors, but it can certainly be worked
with two or four colors. It is five rows wide.

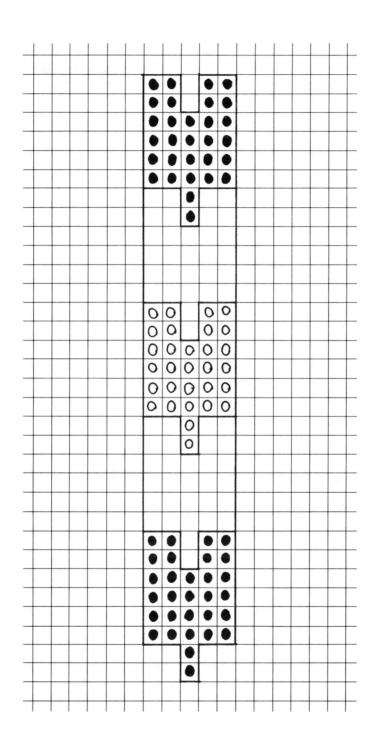

8

CAUCASIAN BORDER

This reverse design was found on a Shirvan Talish (Caucasian) rug. It is worked in three colors with the darkest shade outlining the pattern. There are thirteen rows.

55

9

CHINESE FRET BORDER

This Chinese fret border design, found in many of the Chinese crafts, has the effect of overlapping waves. It requires fourteen rows and is easily adjusted by moving the top or bottom rows.

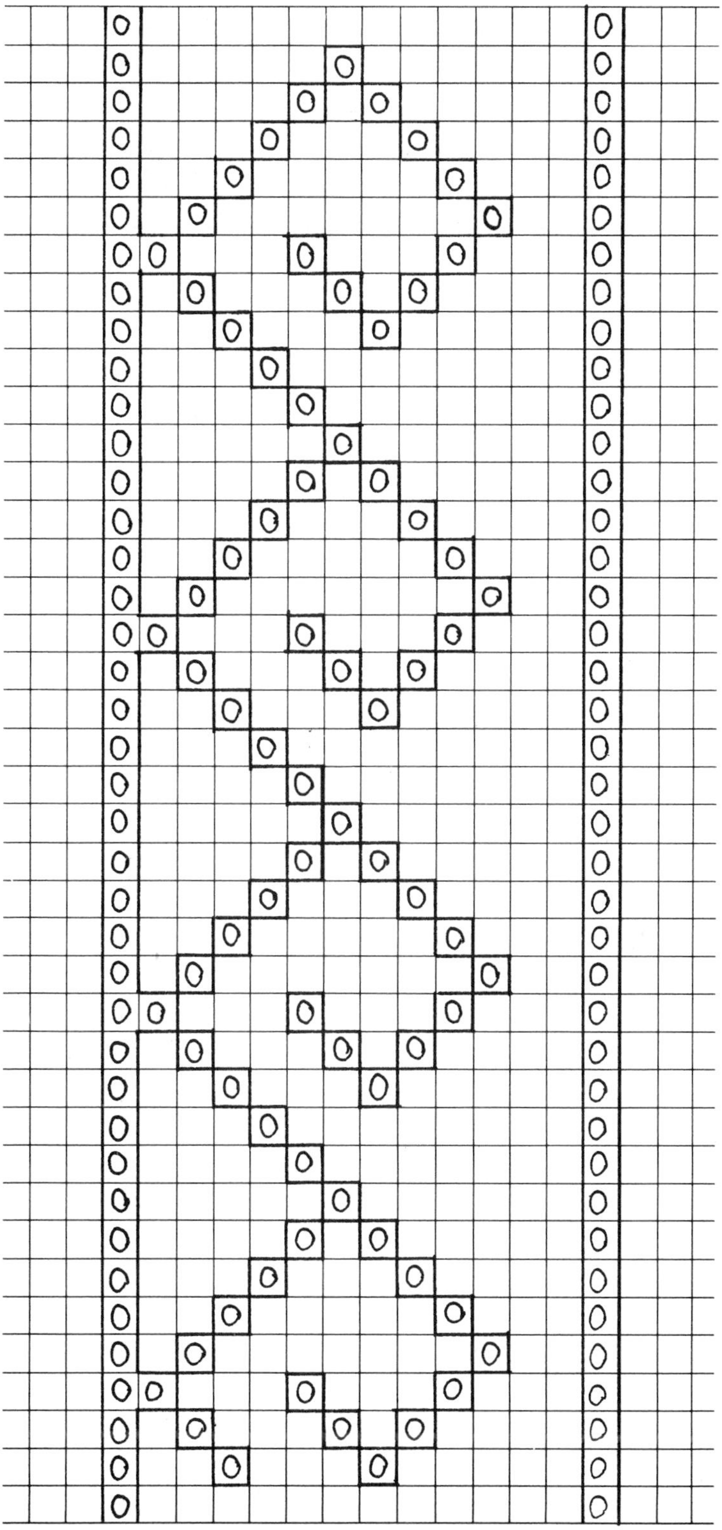

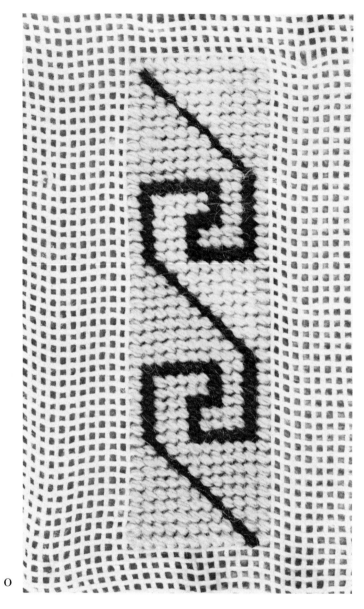

10

Chinese Fret Border

Another Chinese border design that has been found in other cultures. It is also called the Greek Fret. This border has many variations that can be arrived at by simply changing the interior design. Add a stitch to the upper portion of the key, and the design becomes reversible.

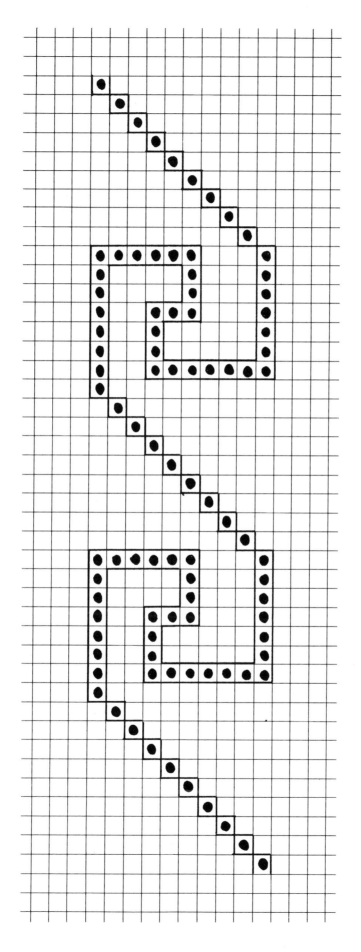

1 1

Chippewa Indian Border

Chippewa (Ojibwa) Indian border used on birch bark. Adapted for needlepoint, it uses four colors. It is ten rows wide.

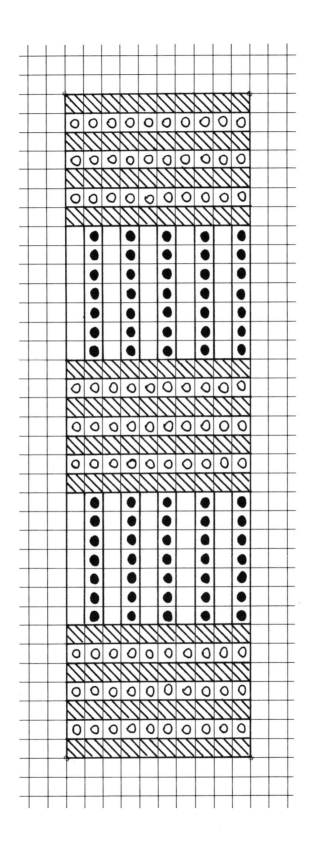

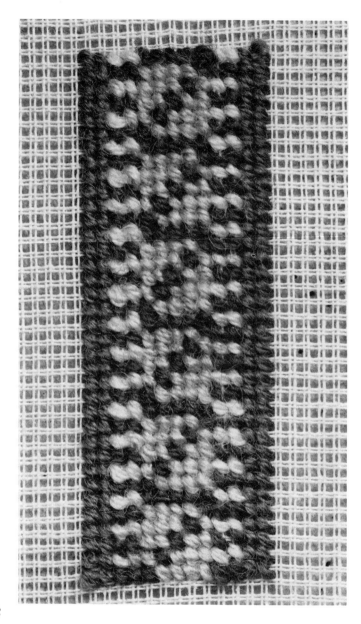

1 2

Chippewa Indian Border

This Chippewa Indian border design is most effective when done in three colors. It is thirteen rows wide.

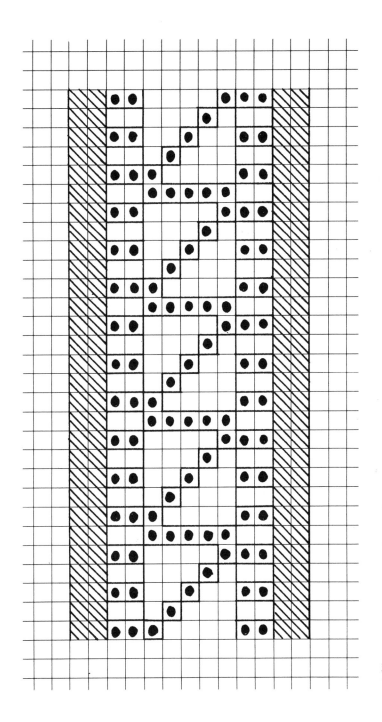

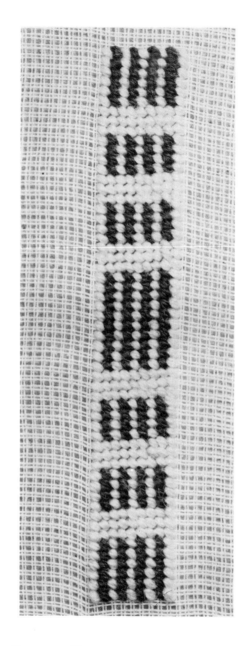

13

CHIPPEWA INDIAN BORDER

This Chippewa Indian birch-bark design uses dark and light contrasting colors. It is nine rows wide.

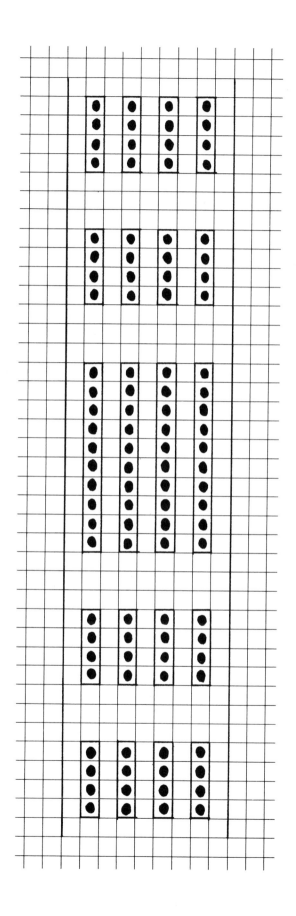

Chippewa Indian Border

This Chippewa Indian design was found on a reed mat. It requires nineteen rows in width. Since the repeat pattern is so large, count carefully before starting a new repeat. This border design can also be used as a center (see Plate 6).

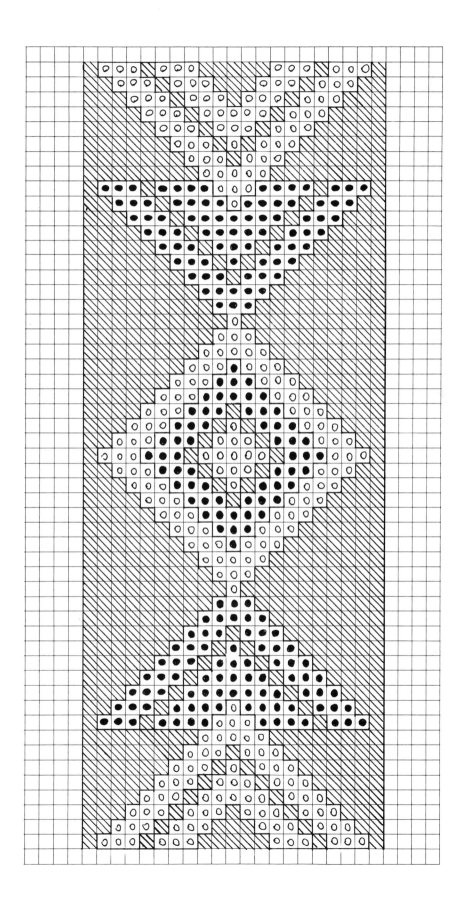

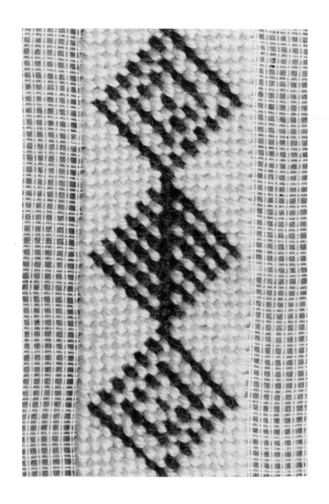

CONGOLESE BORDER

A woven mat from the African Lower Congo inspired this interesting border. It is thirteen rows wide.

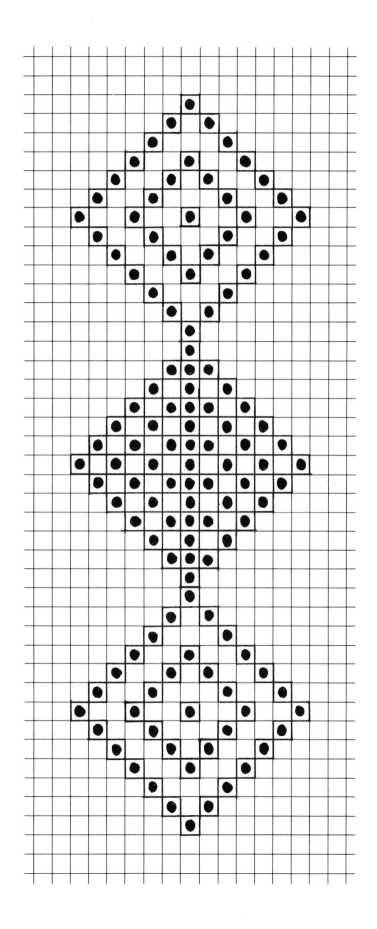

16

Congolese Border

This design was found on a Belgian Congo wall decoration. It requires thirteen rows in addition to the outer borders.

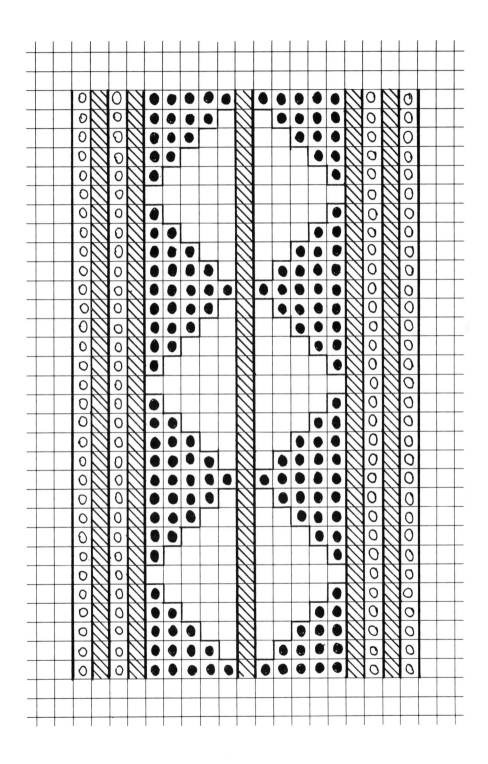

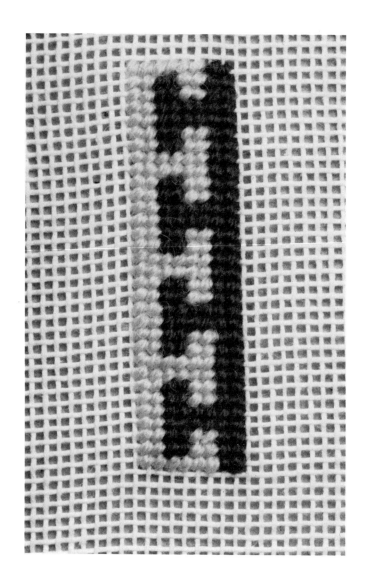

17

Dutch Border

This reverse pattern was actually found on a piece of Dutch embroidery. It frequently appears on rugs of Oriental origin. It can be done in two contrasting colors, and it is eight rows wide.

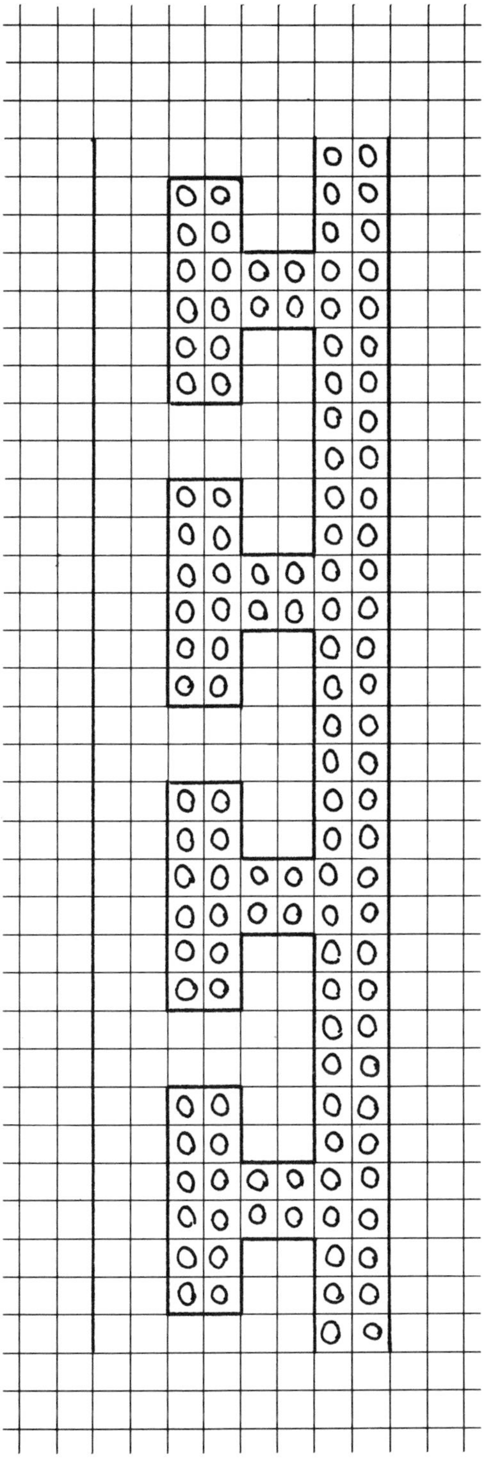

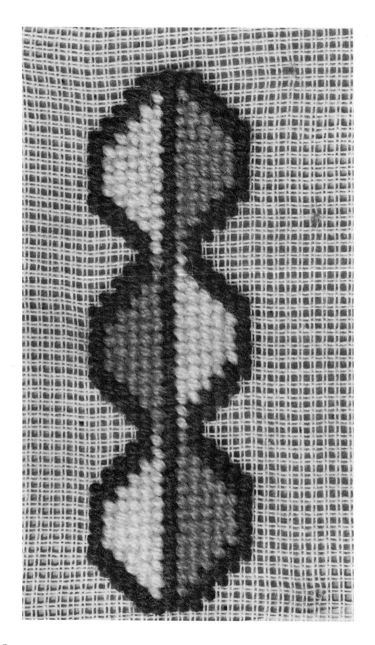

18

DUTCH BORDER

A simple border adapted from Dutch embroidery. Notice the
alternating color pattern. It is thirteen rows wide.

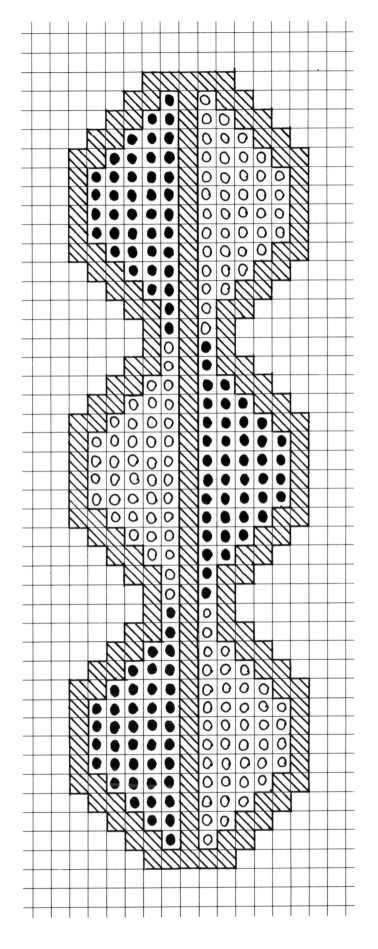

19

Dutch Border

This border is done in three colors. It consists of fourteen rows.

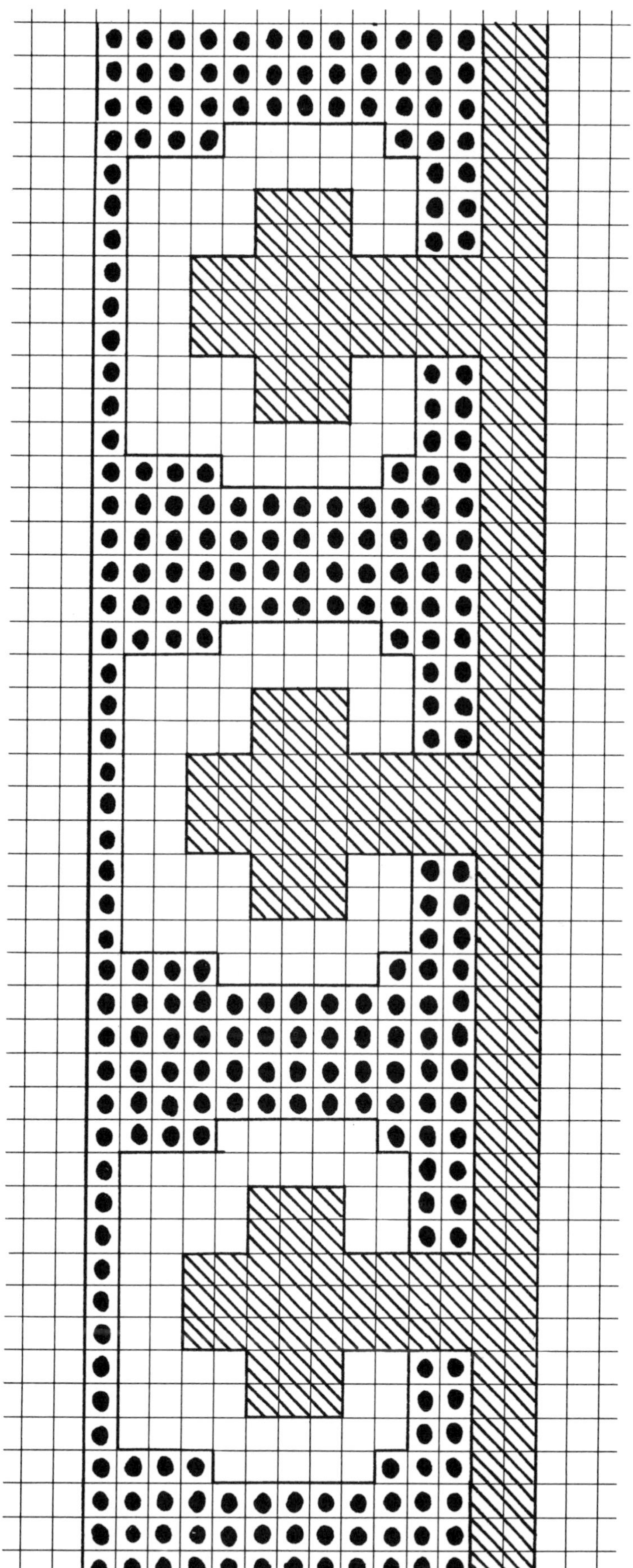

2 0

GREEK BORDER

Adapted from Greek peasant embroidery, this checkerboard
pattern would be at home in any culture. If you aren't lazy, try
this one with a one-stitch center of the opposite color in each
square.

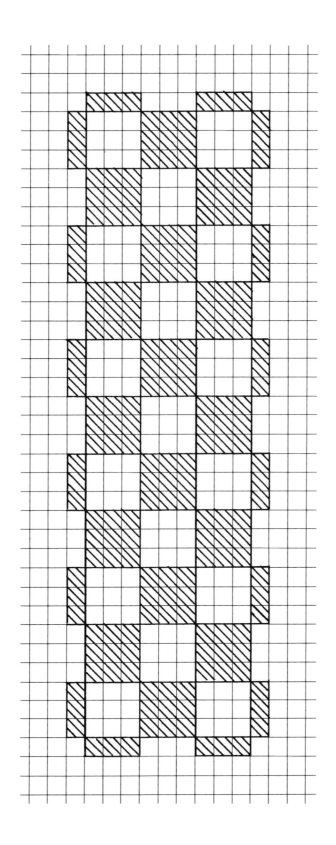

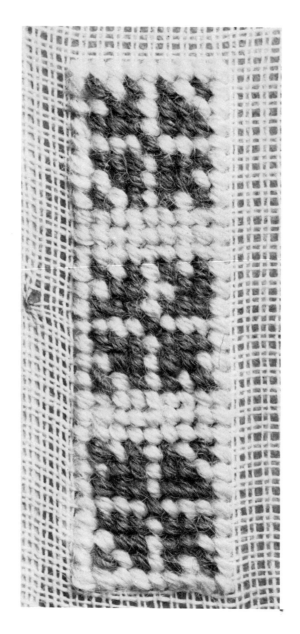

2 1

GREEK BORDER

A lovely border of Greek origin. It is usually worked in one color
but should look just as charming in alternating colors or even
random colors all around. Seven rows wide, with a single stitch
border.

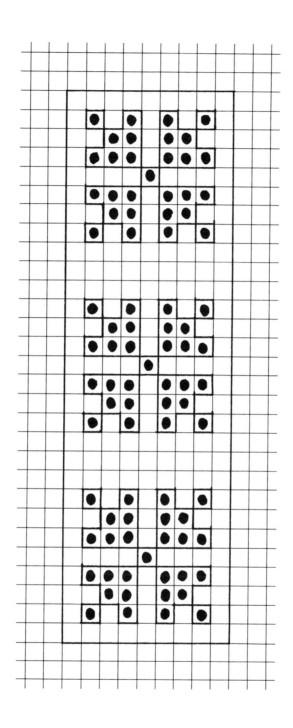

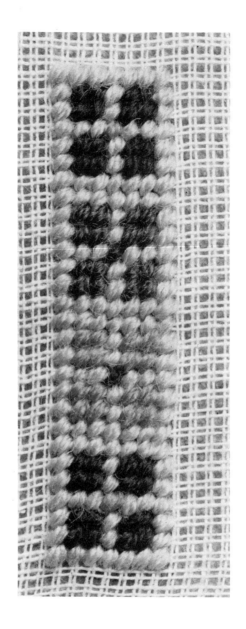

2 2

GREEK BORDER

This Greek embroidery design worked in different colors will use up those odd bits of wool in a nice way. It requires five rows, with a single stitch border.

23

GREEK BORDER

Adapted from Greek peasant embroidery, this border is done in
three colors. It requires fourteen rows.

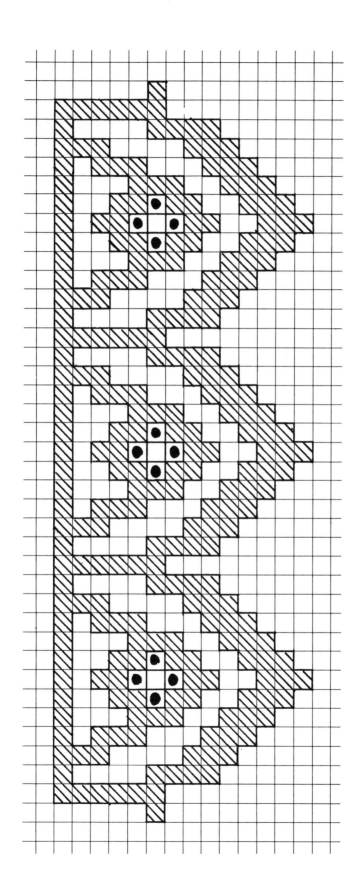

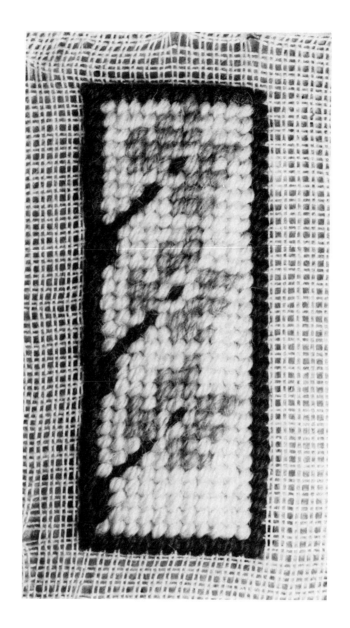

24

GREEK BORDER

From Greece, this delicate flower border may be worked in many different colors. It is another good border for using up odds and ends of yarn. It requires thirteen rows.

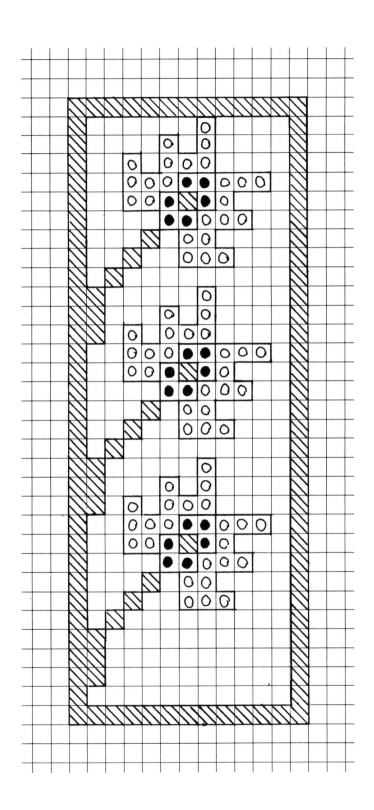

2 5

GREEK BORDER

This is a typical Greek peasant embroidery design. Outline in
one color; fill in design and background in second color. It is
eighteen rows wide, with a single line edge.

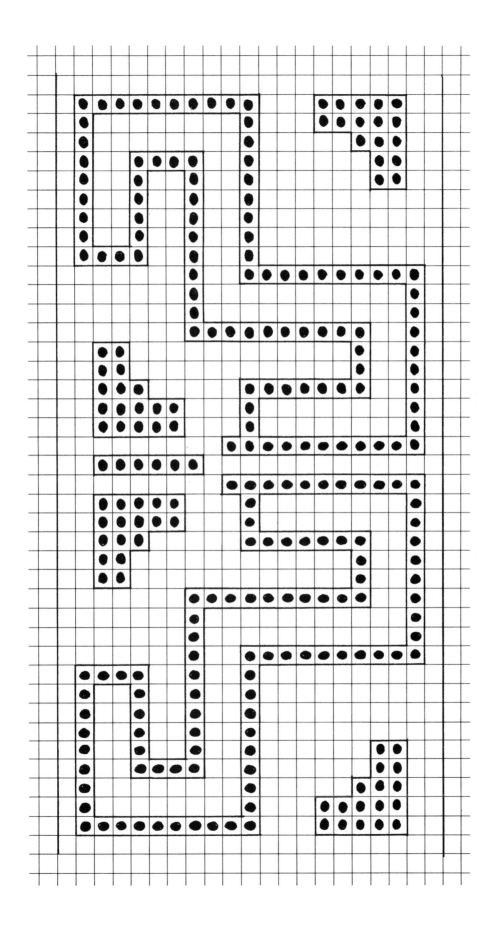

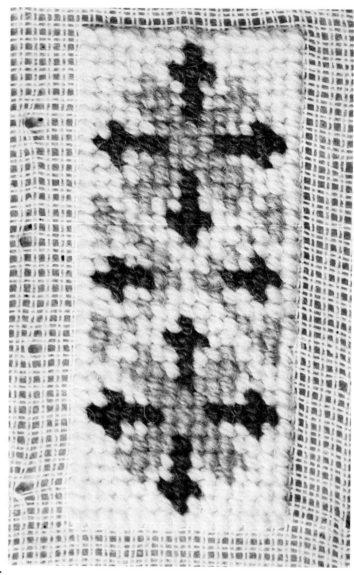

2 6

Greek Border

Found on a Greek hand-embroidered blouse, this charming
border is usually done in two colors on a pale background. It is
thirteen rows wide, plus one row on each side.

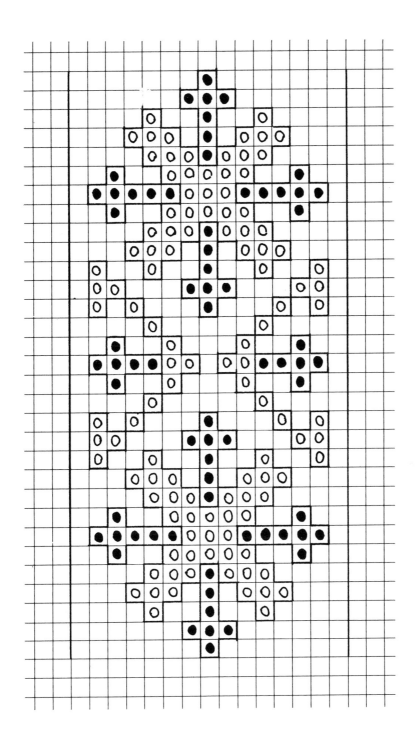

27

Japanese Stencil Border

This design was taken from a most unusual art form, the Japanese stencil-cutting. It has been used primarily in the decoration of cotton or crepe dress fabrics. Note the simple use of the single stitch, the L shape, and the cross. Shown here as seventeen rows, it has many possible variations both in length and width.

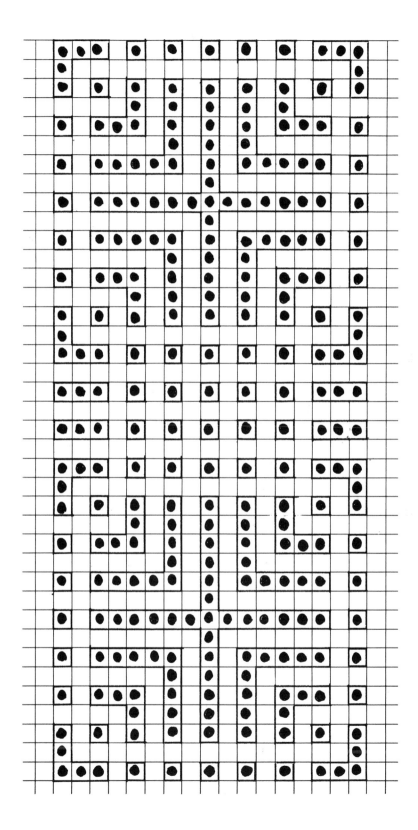

28

JAPANESE BORDER

This Japanese border is a simple single-line design repetitively worked. It was found on blue and white Japanese porcelain planting pot. Fourteen rows are required for this border.

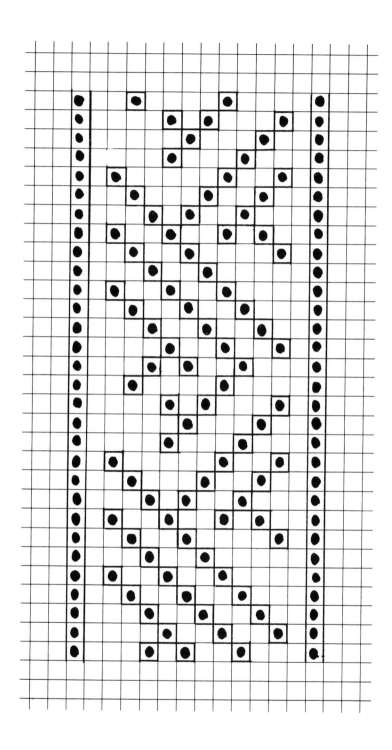

95

29

Mexican Border

This ancient Mexican border design is usually worked in one color against a contrasting background. You might want to try using different colors for each repeat. This border has a fifteen-stitch width plus one row on either side.

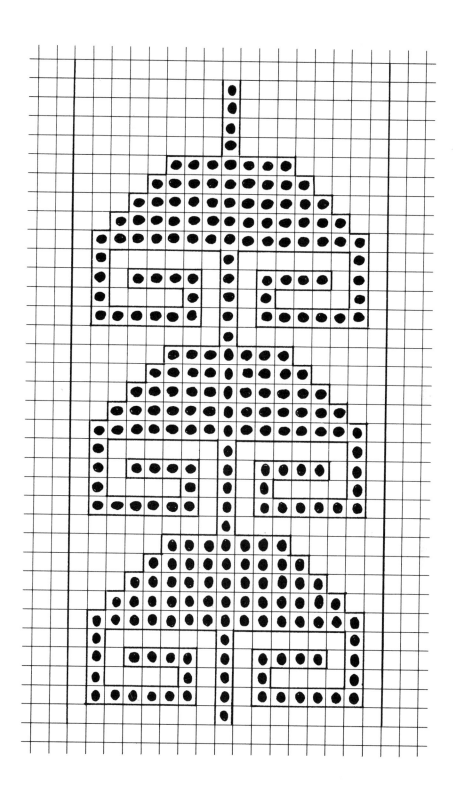

30

MEXICAN BORDER

An ancient Mexican flat stamp from Guerrero inspired this border. Stitched in one color on a pale background, it requires twelve rows.

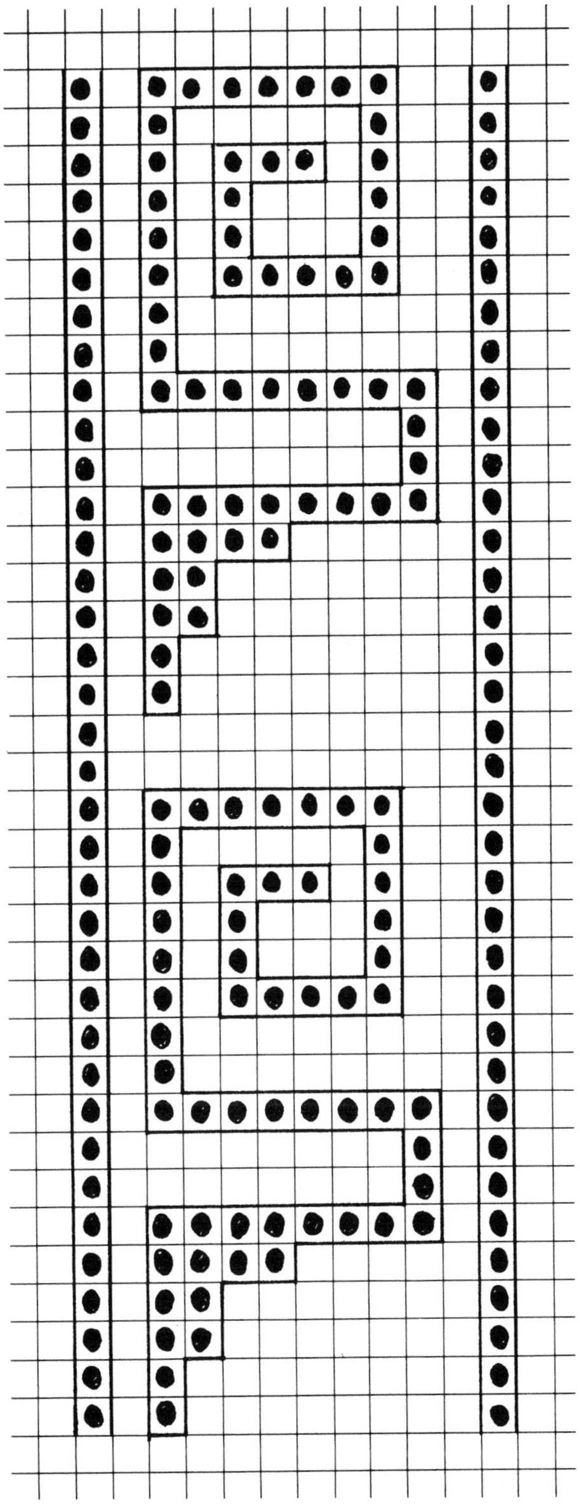

3 [1]

MEXICAN BORDER

This ancient Mexican border is complicated but worth the effort.
Notice that the needlework sample reverses position of every
other repeat pattern. Done in one color against a pale
background. Requires eleven rows.

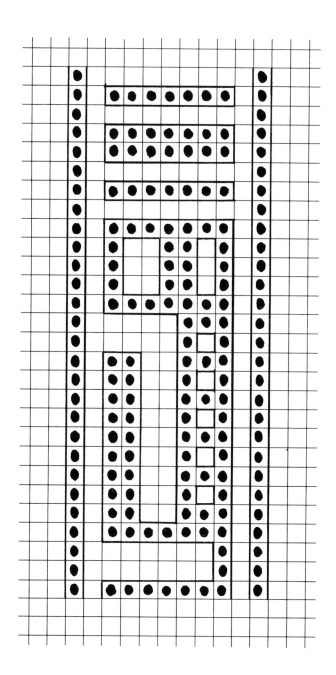

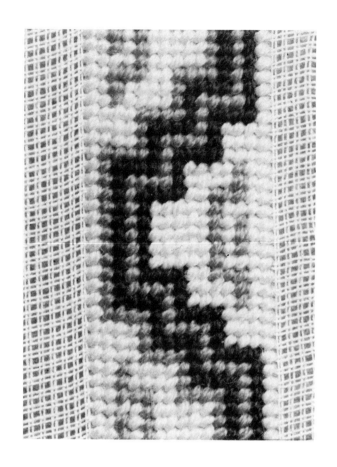

3 2

Mexican Border

This is a traditional Mexican step pattern. Shown here in two
colors on a light background, it can be worked in four tones of
one color or in four different colors. It requires thirteen rows
in addition to the outer borders.

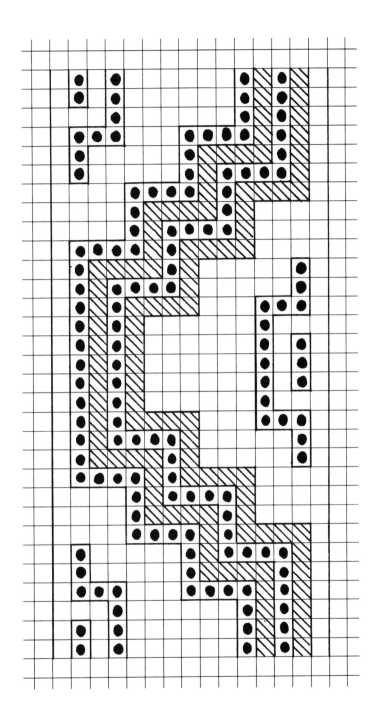

33

Norwegian Border

Simple Norwegian border adapted from a knitted sweater. Done in three colors; five rows wide.

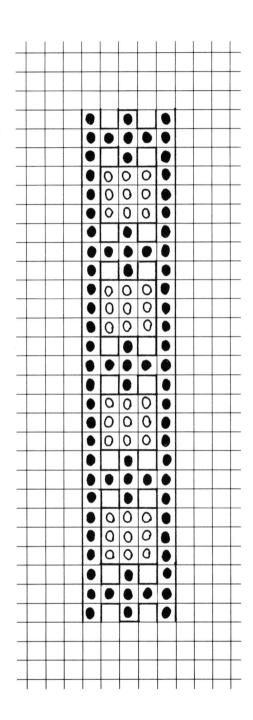

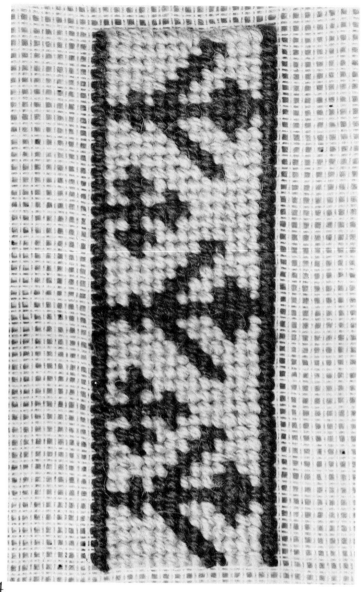

34

NORWEGIAN BORDER

This design was found on a delicate piece of Norwegian embroidery. Shown here in two colors, it can also be done by having the flower in a third color and the leaves in a fourth color. It requires thirteen rows in addition to the outer borders.

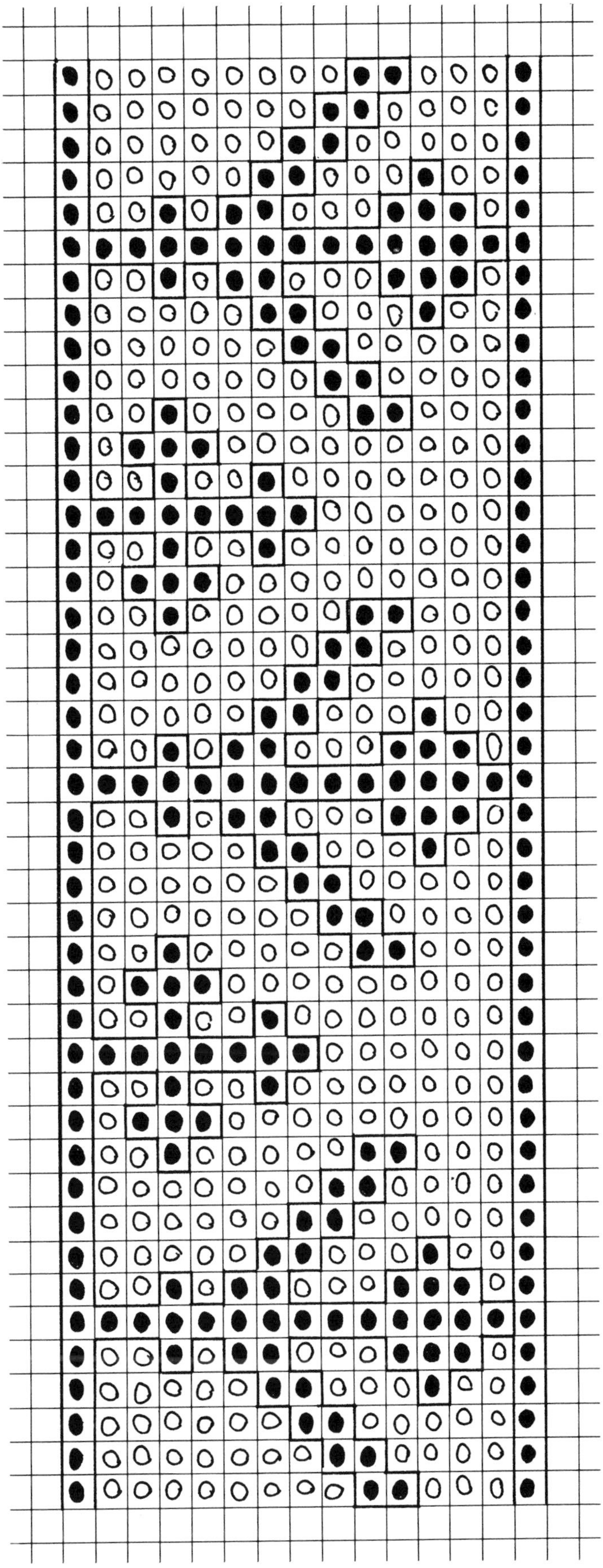

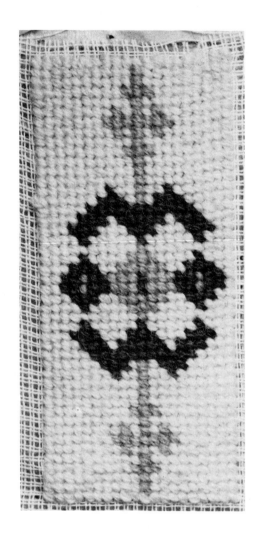

35

Norwegian Border

This Norwegian design is shown here in three colors but can easily be changed to four colors (see belt, Plate 16). This border design requires seventeen rows.

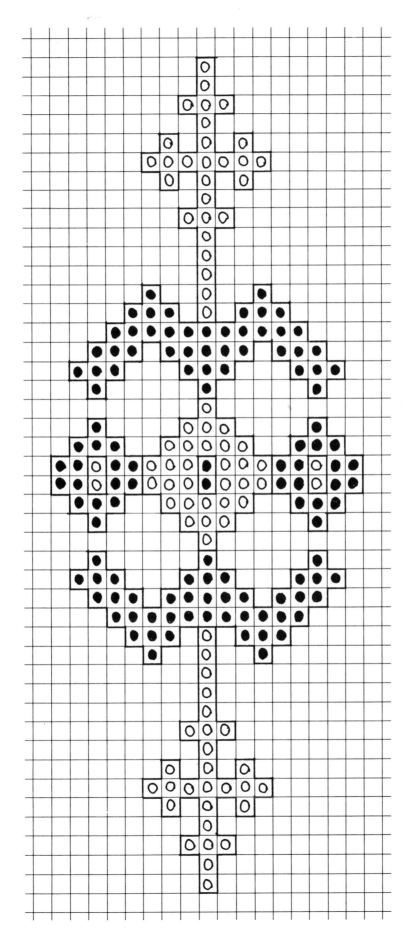

36

ORIENTAL BORDER

This simple nine-row border from an Oriental rug is suitable
for outlining the beginning and end of a series of borders. The
effect can be changed by a rearrangement of dark and light
tones. This versatile border can be made larger by the addition
of a fourth row of the center color or made narrower by using
only two rows of the center color and one rather than two
rows of the end color.

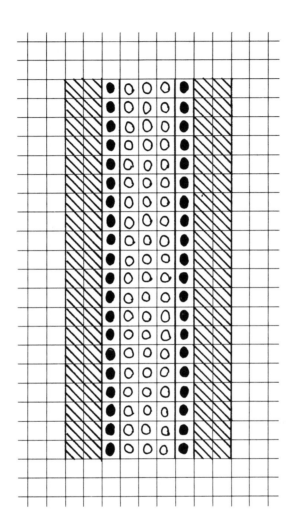

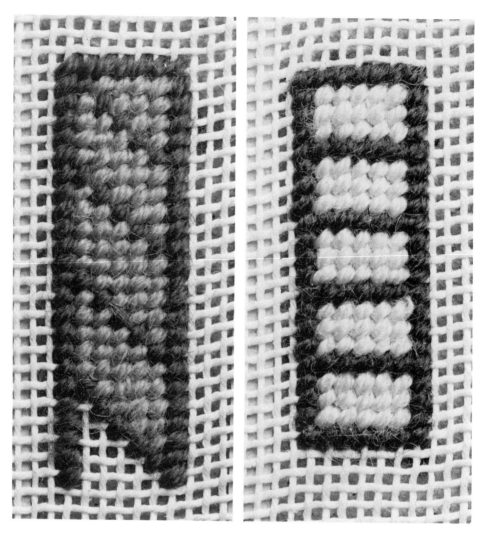

37 and 38

ORIENTAL BORDERS

Here are two simple very effective designs from an old Oriental
rug. Adjustments are simple on these designs. Just change
the width by adding or subtracting from the number of rows
between repeats. These borders may be repeated two or three
times in an overall scheme. Remember that diagonal lines look
different depending upon which way you slant, as all stitches
must go in the same direction.

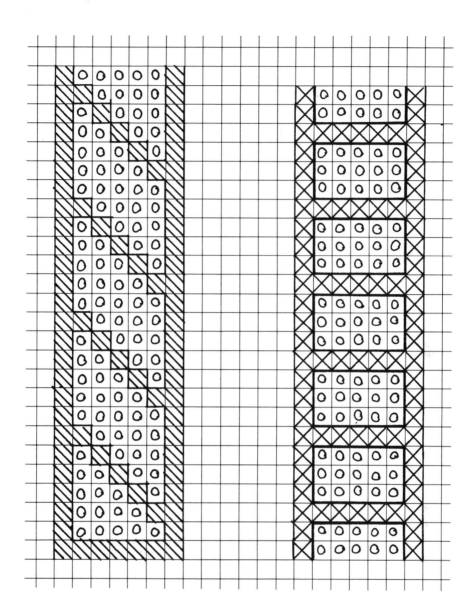

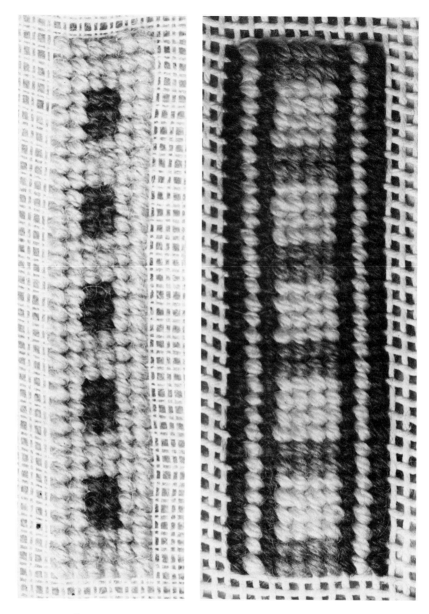

39 and 40

Oriental Borders

These simple borders are usually found between major borders
on Oriental rugs. They are easily adaptable to changes in width
or color combinations.

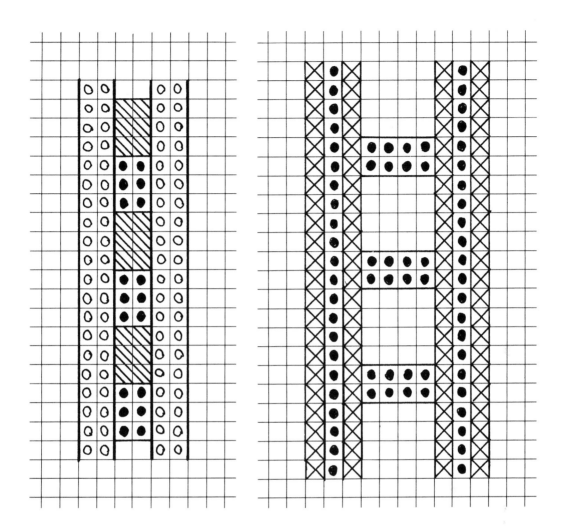

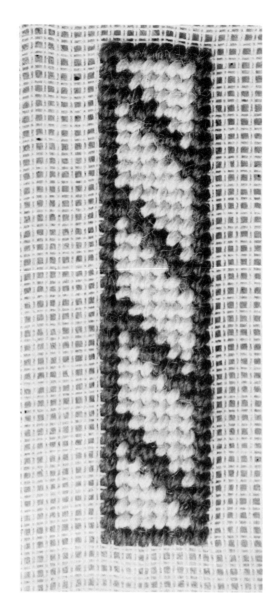

4 ¹

ORIENTAL BORDER

A typical Oriental rug border done in two colors. It is easily
changed to fit your needs by adding or subtracting rows from
the width or length. Instead of a two-six repeat you might try a
two-four or a three-eight repeat. Instead of eight rows in width,
it could be six or thirteen.

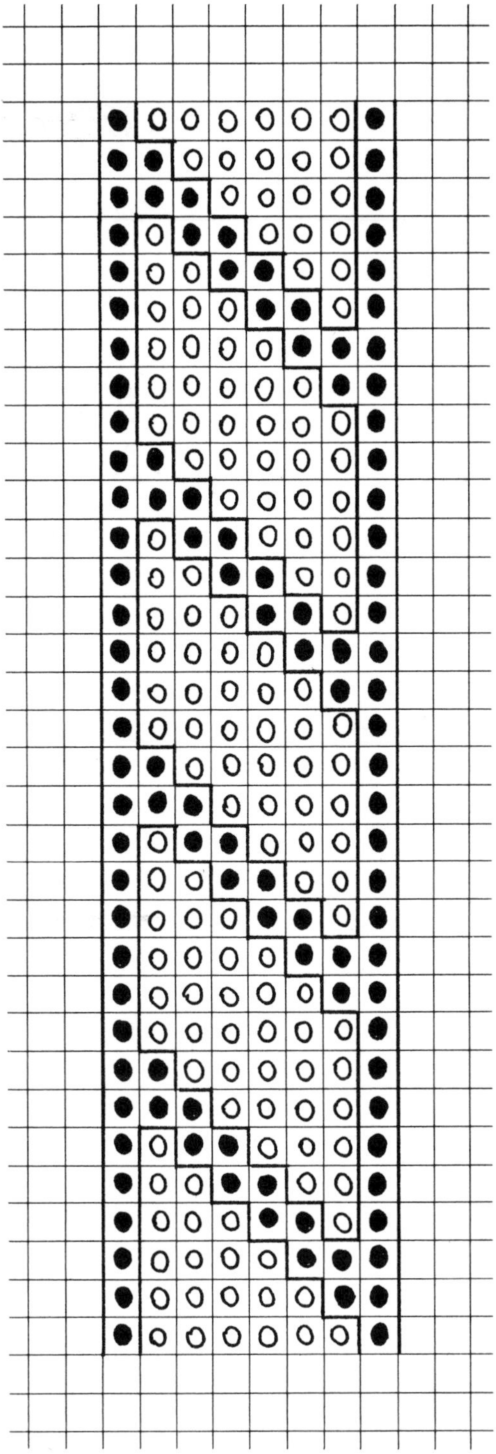

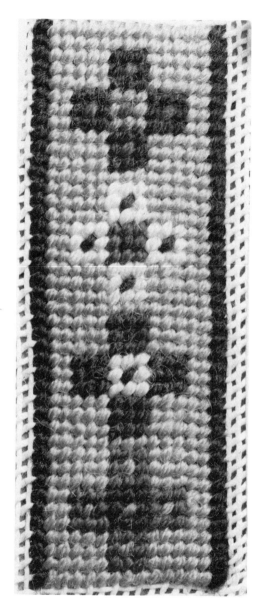

42

Oriental Border

The effort involved in changing colors frequently is worth the trouble. This border is a classic in Oriental rug design. The lack of a consistent repeat of color combinations lends much to the beauty of this border. Including outer borders, this design consists of fifteen rows.

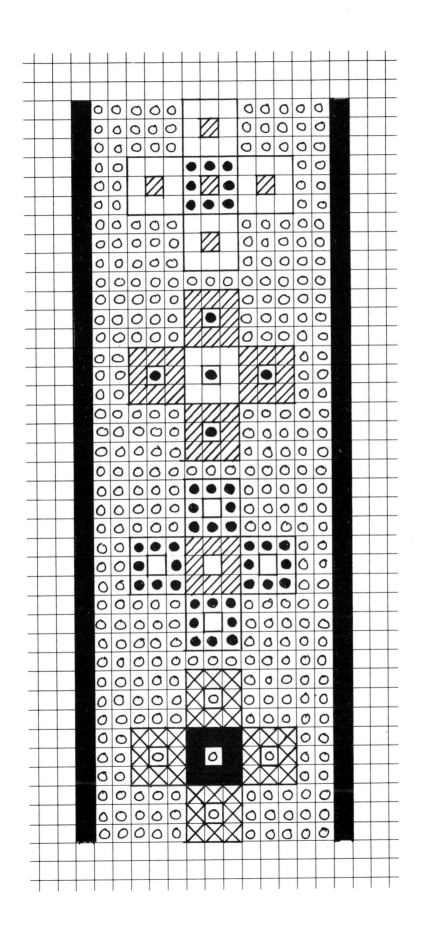

119

43

PERSIAN BORDER

This design is often used in Oriental rugs made in Iran. The simple reverse border is worked in two colors as shown. It is five rows wide.

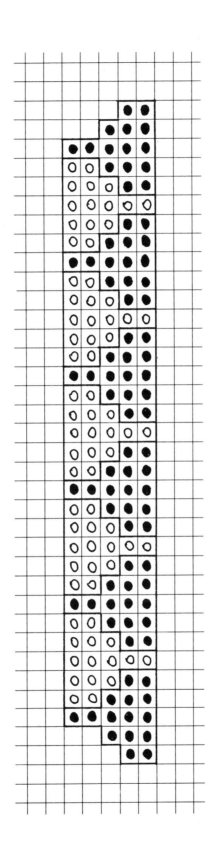

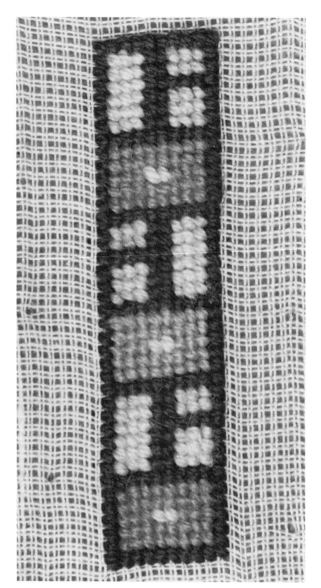

44

PERSIAN BORDER

This Oriental rug border design is of Persian origin. The
effectiveness of this design lies in the contrast between the dark
color outlining each rectangle and the light color repeated inside
the three small rectangles. The colors in the large rectangle do
not have to follow any pattern of repeat (see rug colors, Plate 20).
This border is ten rows wide.

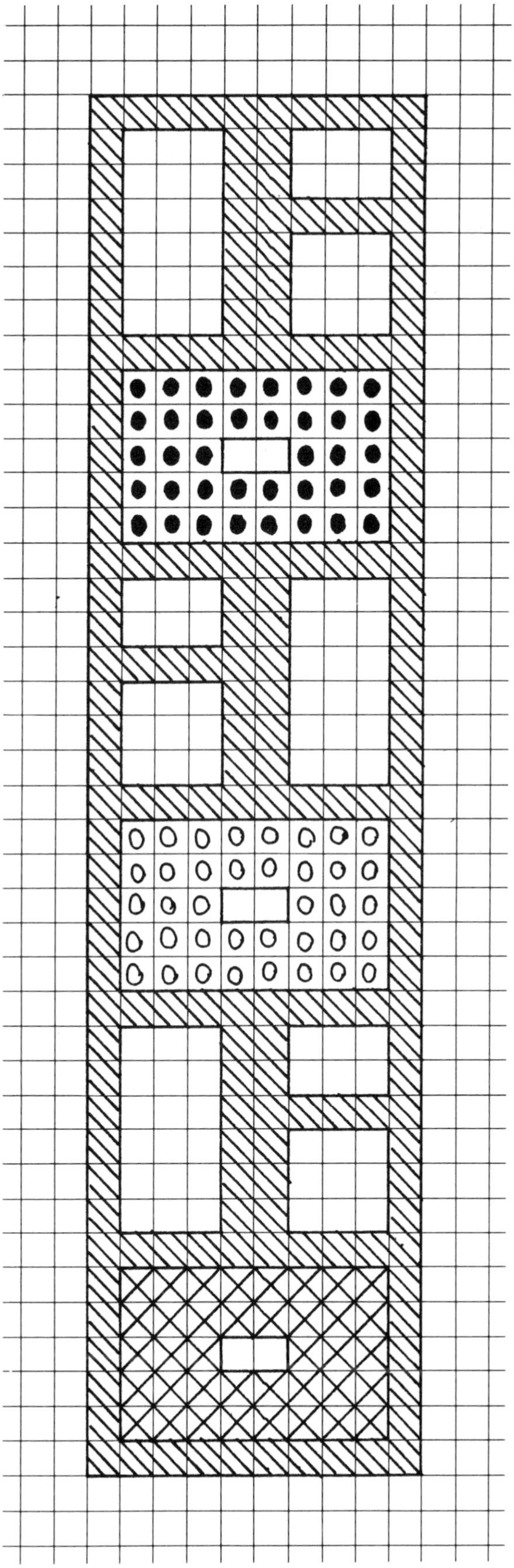

45

PERSIAN BORDER

Adapted from an antique Persian rug, this border makes a lovely belt. See Plate 16, where it was worked on #16 canvas.

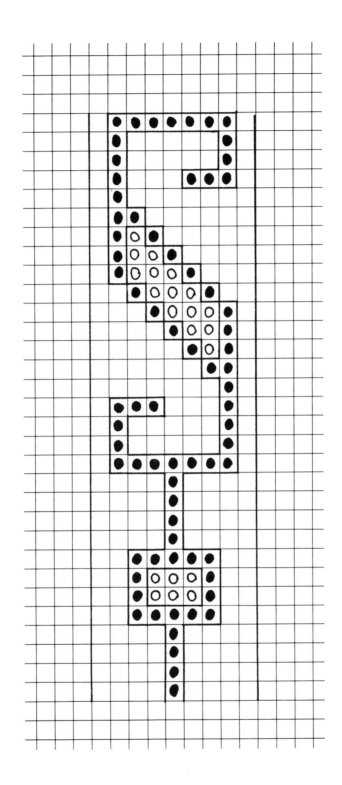

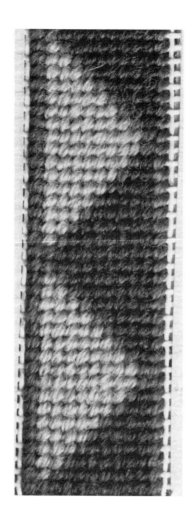

4 6

PERSIAN BORDER

This striking border was found on a Kurdish Kelim rug from
Iran. It is done in three colors, one for outlining, the other two
used on each side of the border. You can change the width of
the border by increasing or decreasing the number of stitches
on each diagonal.

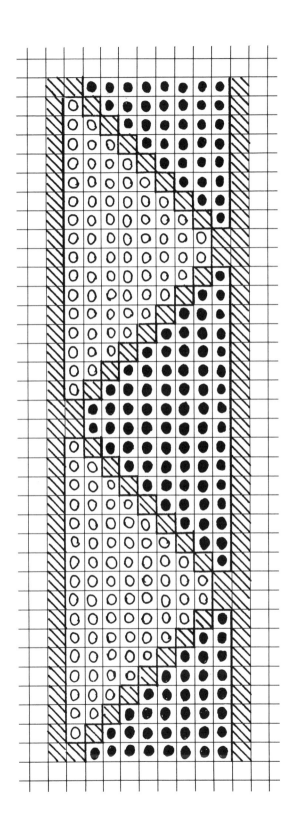

47

Persian Border

An antique Persian rug inspired this border. The colors change
frequently with no set pattern of color repeat. Difficult at first try,
this border is worth the effort involved. (See rug, Plate 20.)
It requires twenty-one rows and is shown with a six stitch edge
on each side.

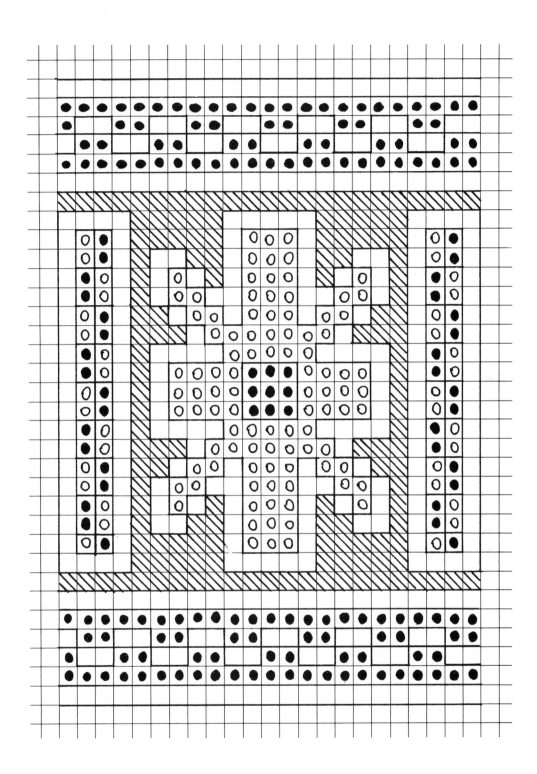

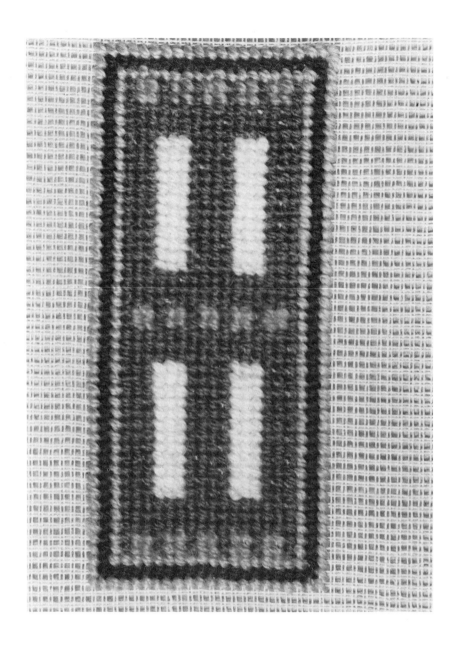

48

SIOUX INDIAN BORDER

This Sioux Indian band was used on robes. The border is done
in three colors and requires sixteen rows plus outside borders.
Watch your corners on this one; each full repeat takes forty-four
stitches.

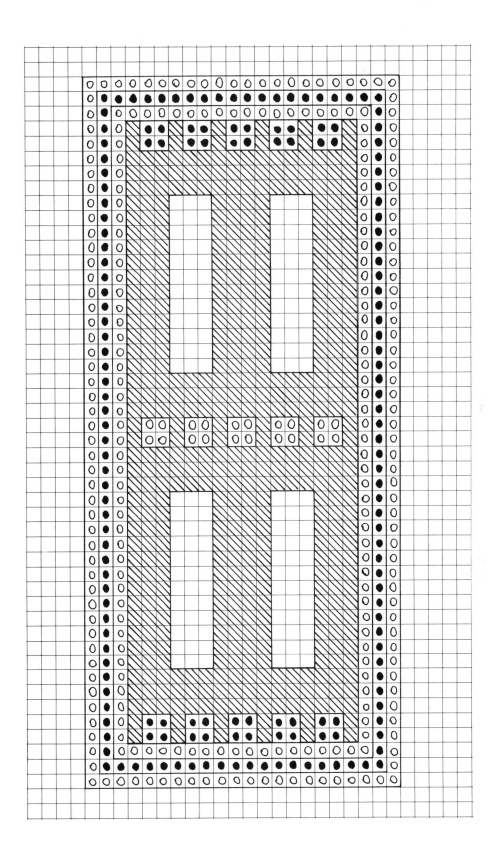

131

49

Sioux Indian Border

Western Sioux Indian beadwork inspired this attractive border. Notice that background stripes alternate colors. There are twenty-one rows.

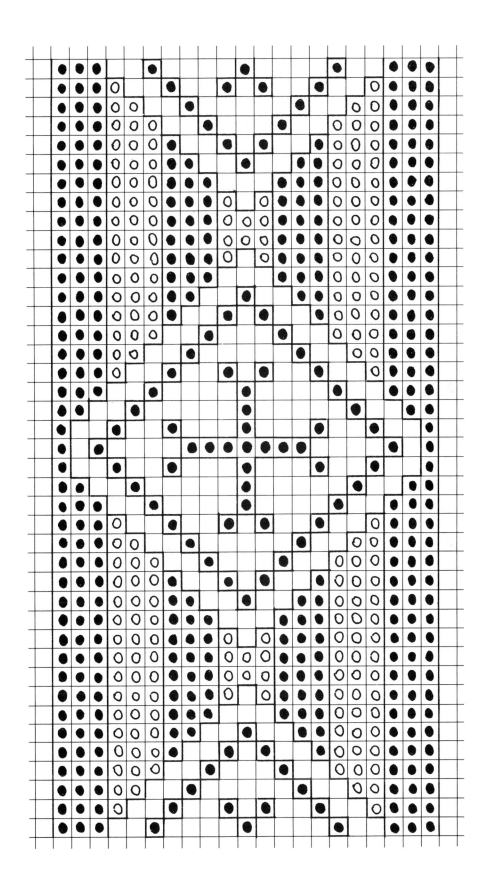

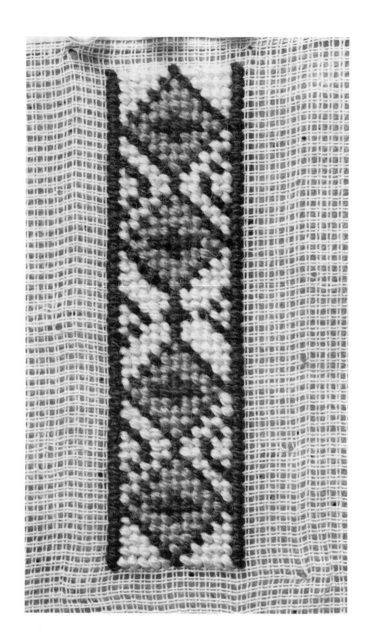

5 0

Sioux Indian Border

Sioux Indian beadwork design shown here for needlepoint in a delicate three-color border. It is thirteen rows wide.

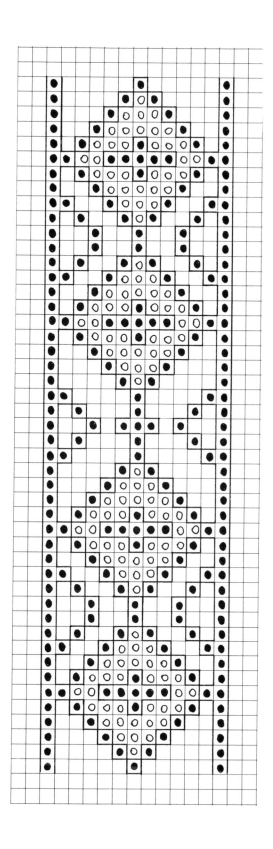

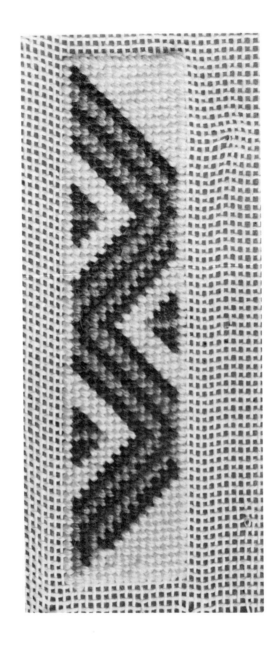

5 [1]

Tanganyikan Border

This African border design was found on a basket from
Tanganyika. This is tricky to do, so start two or three repeats first.
Colors may alternate as shown, or five tones of one color may be
used. It is thirteen rows wide.

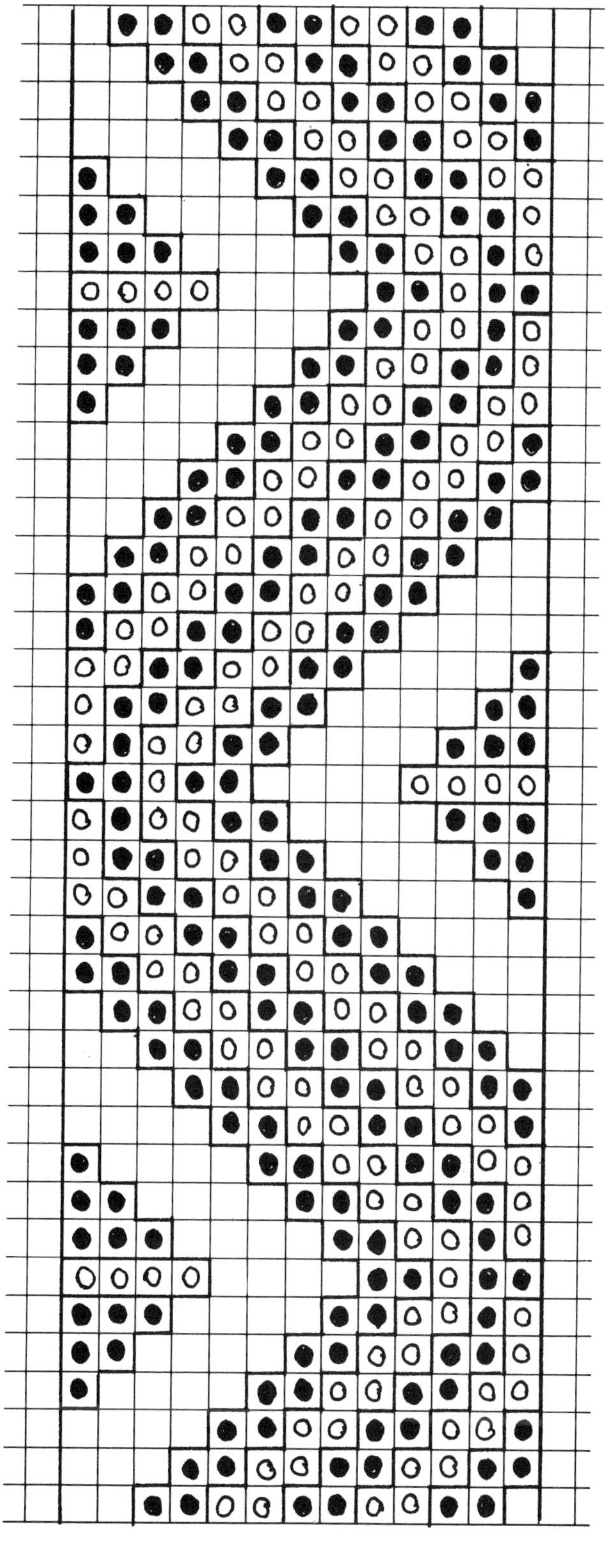

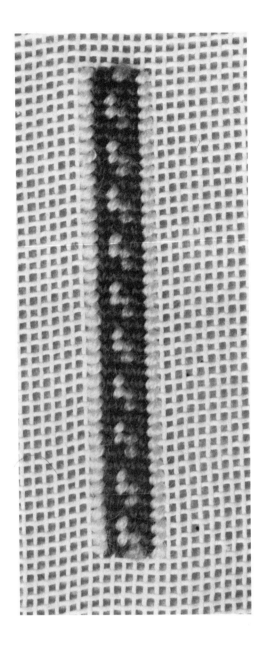

5 2

TURKISH BORDER

A charming border of only six rows, adapted from a Turkish rug. May be used alone or as a frame for a wider border.

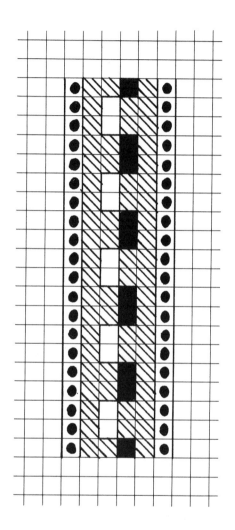

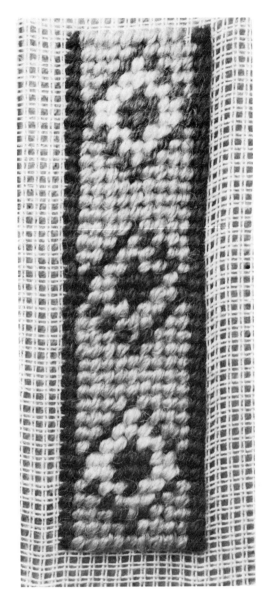

53

Turkish Border

This simple diamond pattern was found on a Turkish rug. It may be used with the same color repeated on each diamond, or two or three different colors may be repeated. It is eleven rows wide.

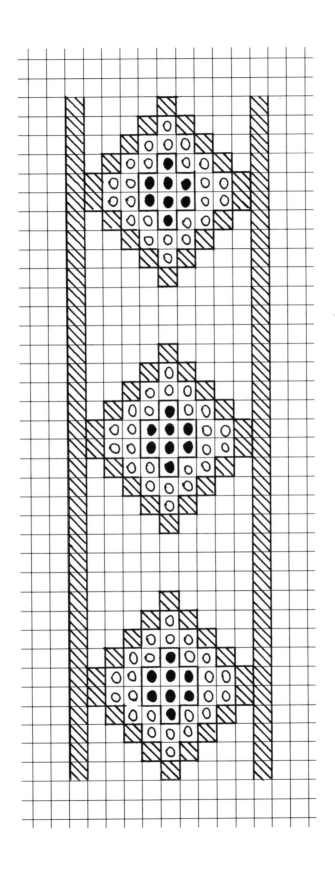

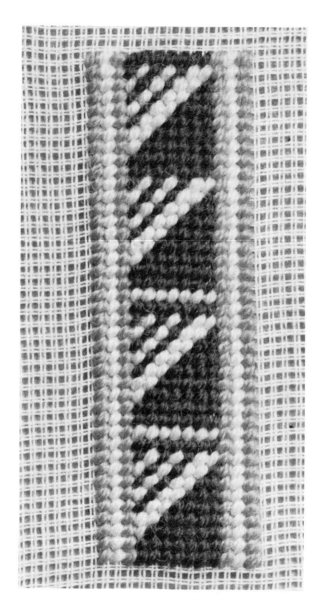

54

YUGOSLAVIAN BORDER

A Yugoslavian border design found on a peasant blouse. It is
usually done with the light color the same throughout and the
remainder repeated in alternating colors. The border is seven
rows wide with three rows bordering each side.

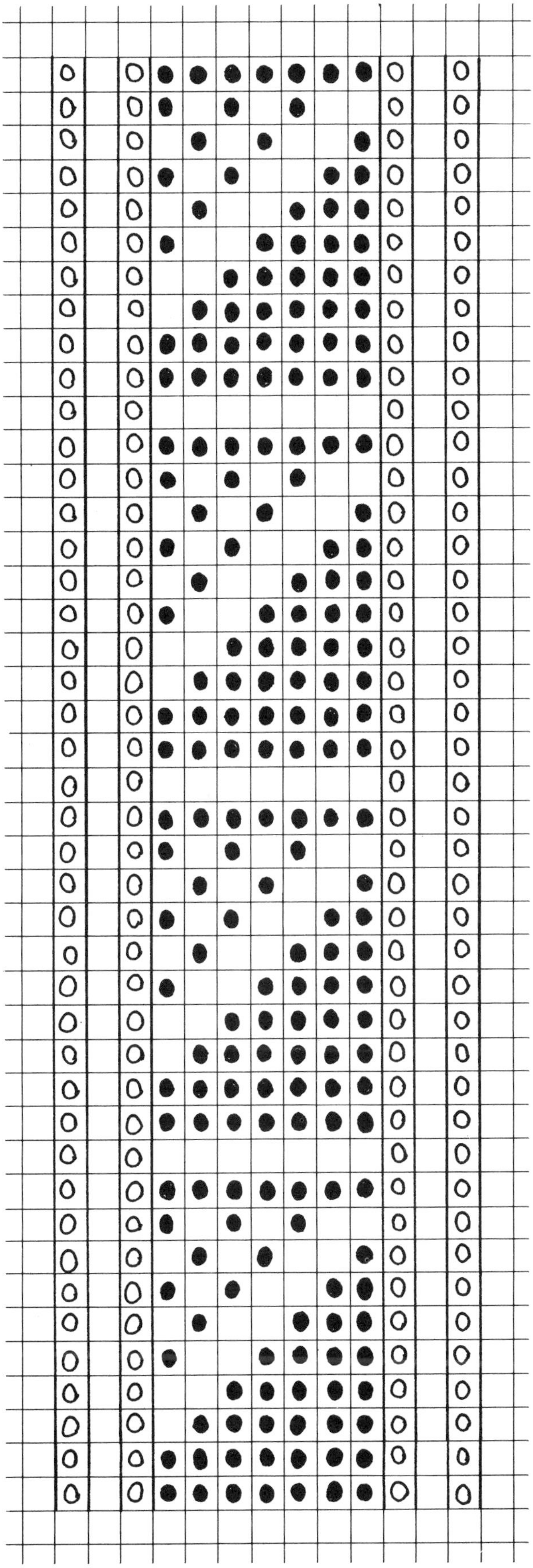

55

ALASKAN INDIAN SCATTER

The Alaskan Tlingit Indians call this the winding around or
tying pattern. Basket-weavers often use this scatter as a narrow
border by just continuing the pattern in a single straight
line as shown.

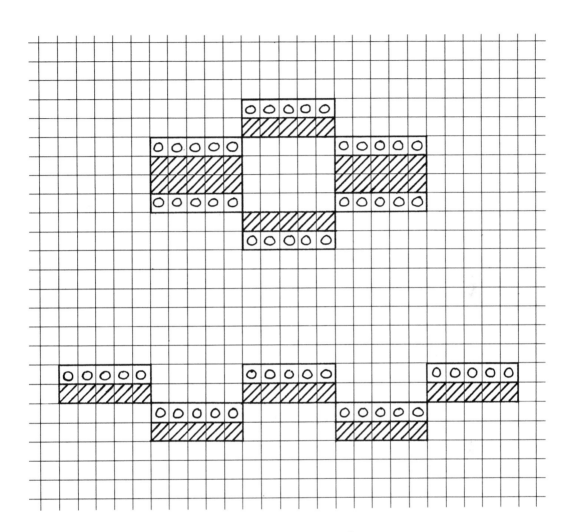

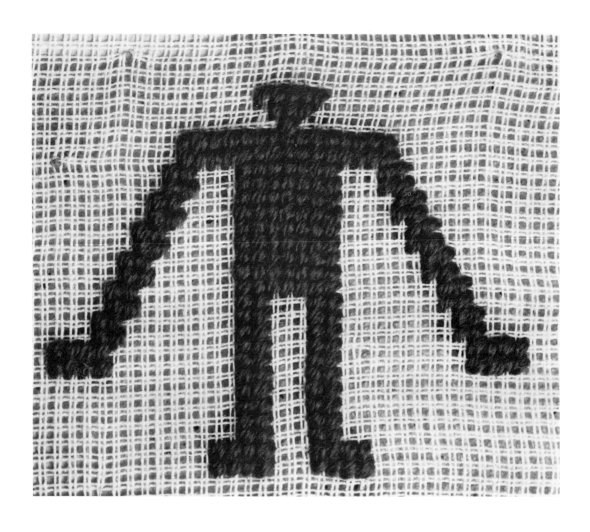

56

ALASKAN INDIAN SCATTER

This delightful man was found on a spruce root basket made by
the Alaskan Tlingit Indians. He can be used on a border for
wall hangings, a scatter design, or on a pillow such as the one
shown in Plate 8. He is twenty-six rows tall.

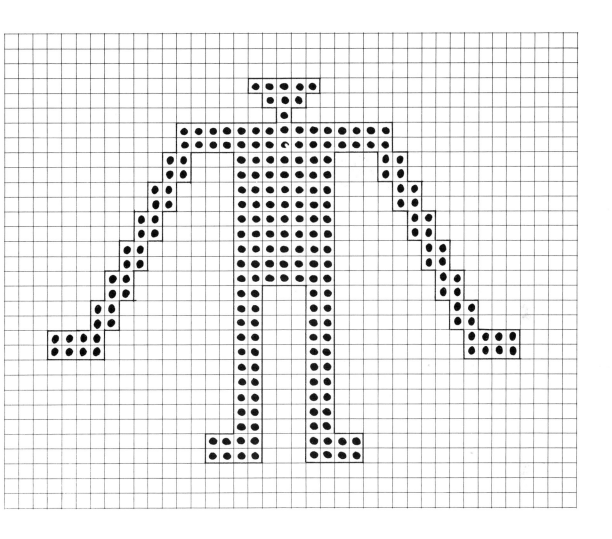

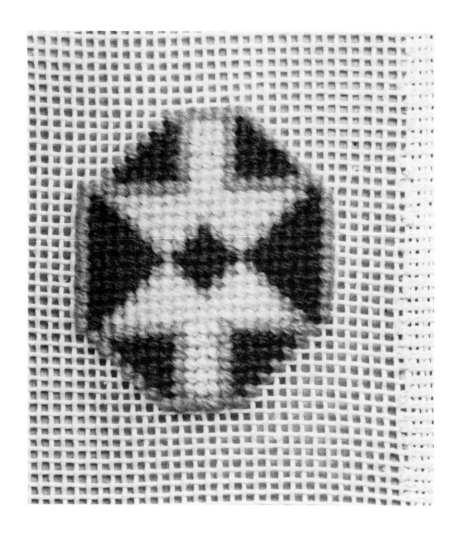

57

Caucasian Scatter

A scatter design of Caucasian origin usually done in three colors. See footstool cover in Plate 15 for the effect of a repeated pattern of this design. It is easily enlarged for use as a main center design.

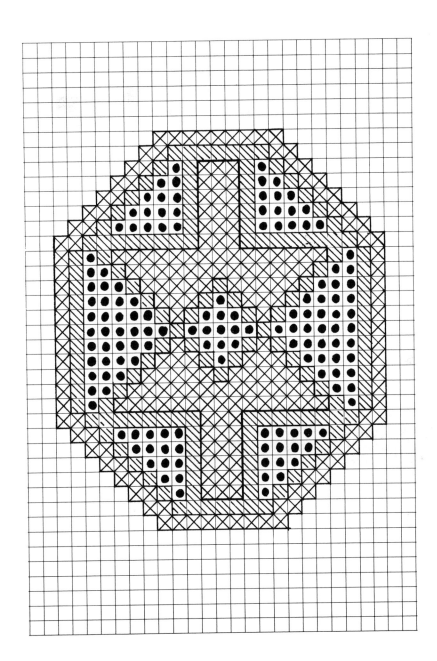

149

58

CHINESE SCATTER

This simple Chinese scatter design was taken from an early blue
and white porcelain bowl on display in the British Museum.
It has many possibilities because of its simplicity and can be used
as a border, in groupings as shown on the graph, or alone.
The design is thirteen rows by seven rows and is easily adjusted
to suit your space requirements.

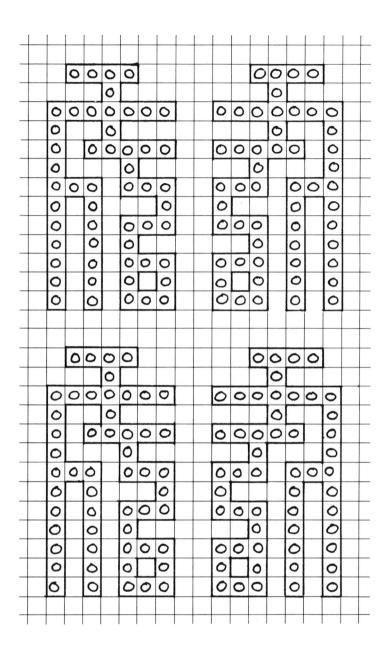

151

59

DUTCH SCATTER

Scatter design adapted from Dutch embroidery sampler. It can be enlarged for a pillow center. I do not recommend this design for a rug center, as it would not maintain its character when enlarged too much.

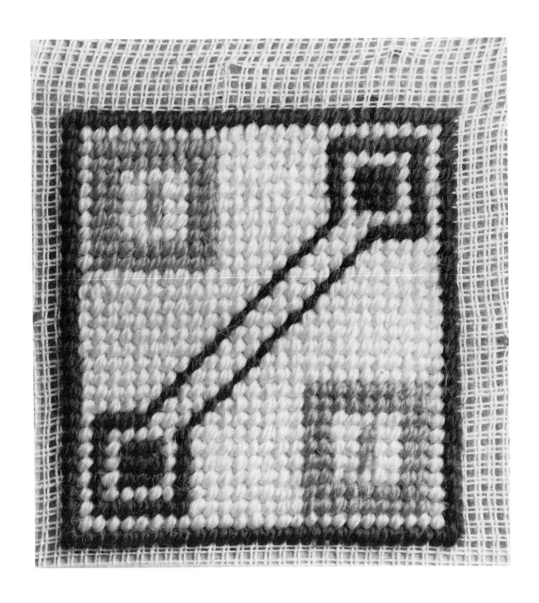

6 o

DUTCH SCATTER

This contemporary Dutch scatter design can be easily enlarged
for a pillow center.

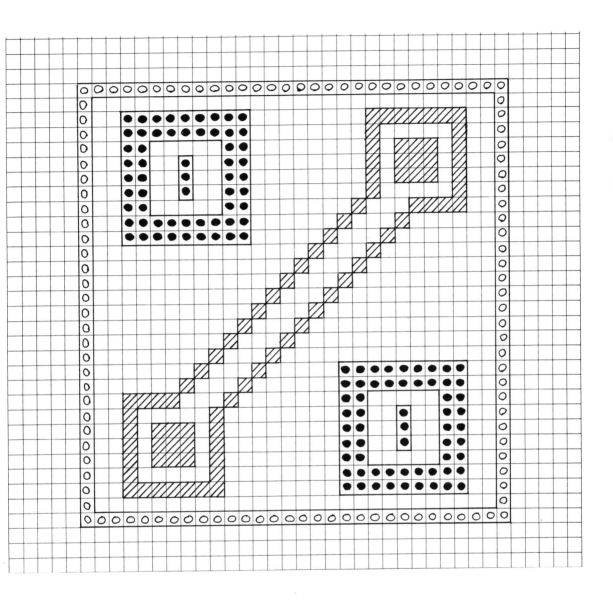

6 1

JAPANESE SCATTER

This Japanese scatter was adapted from a nineteenth-century
Imari bowl. On the original the background was fired in cobalt
blue and the outlines were applied in gold leaf. The design
requires twenty-nine rows each way and has a more authentic
appearance when stitched in two colors.

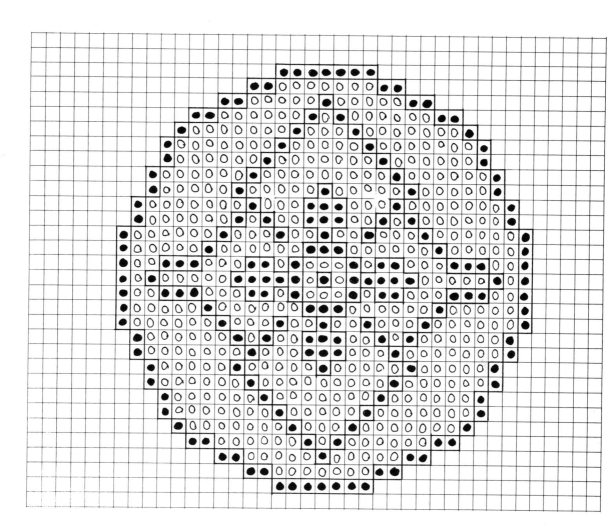

6 2

MEXICAN SCATTER

This delightful scatter design was found on an old Mexican jug.
Shown in one color, it may be worked in two or three colors.

63

NORWEGIAN SCATTER

Norwegian drawn-thread work was adapted here for a
center or scatter design. It is lovely done in a dark color on a pale
background or a pale color on a dark background. See pillow on
page 215 for design worked as a border.

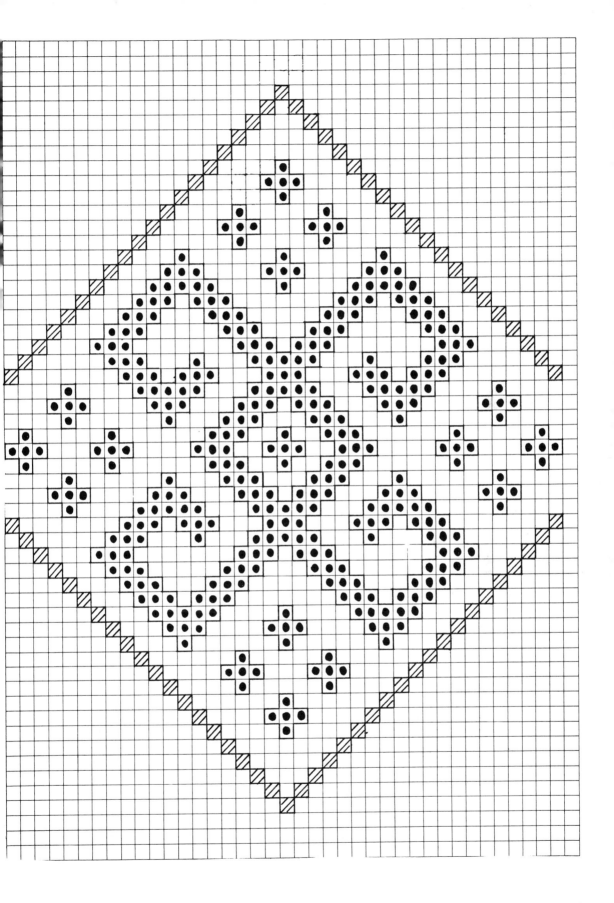

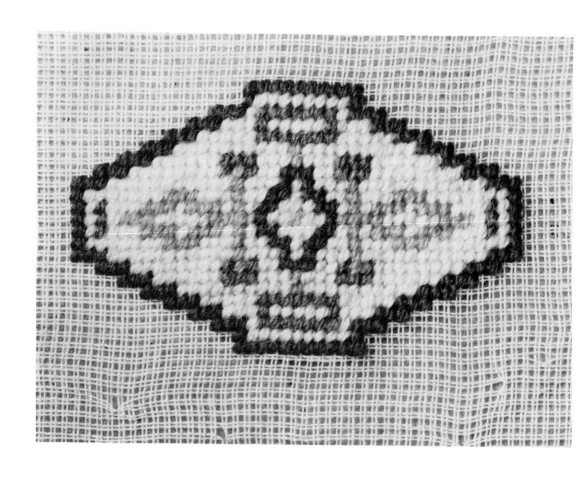

64

ORIENTAL SCATTER

A typical Oriental rug center or scatter design. Used as a scatter,
follow count as shown. For a pillow center, double each box.
For a rug center, count each box as four stitches.

6 5

PERSIAN SCATTER

An antique rug from Iran inspired this interesting design. It
can be used as a pillow center or a scatter on a rug. (See Plate 20.)

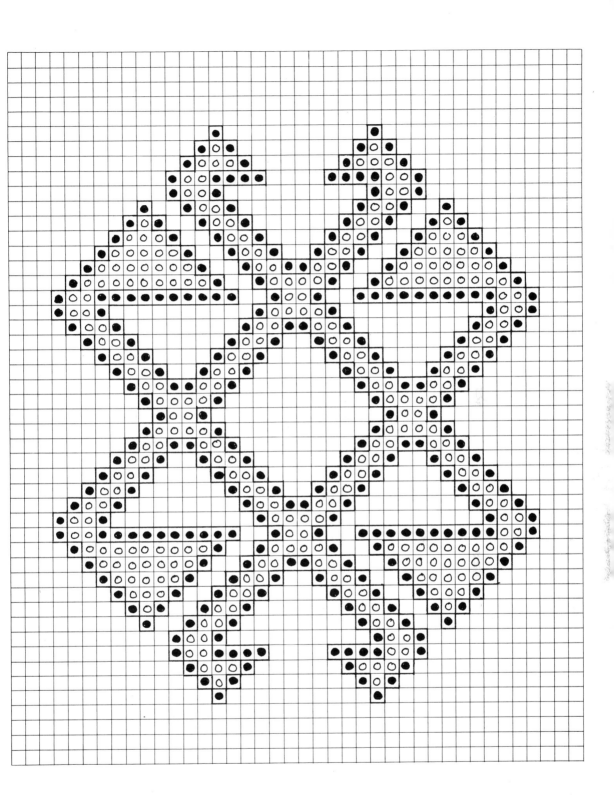

66

PERSIAN SCATTER

An antique rug from Iran inspired this scatter design. It can be
enlarged for a pillow or rug center very nicely. It consists of
twenty-five rows.

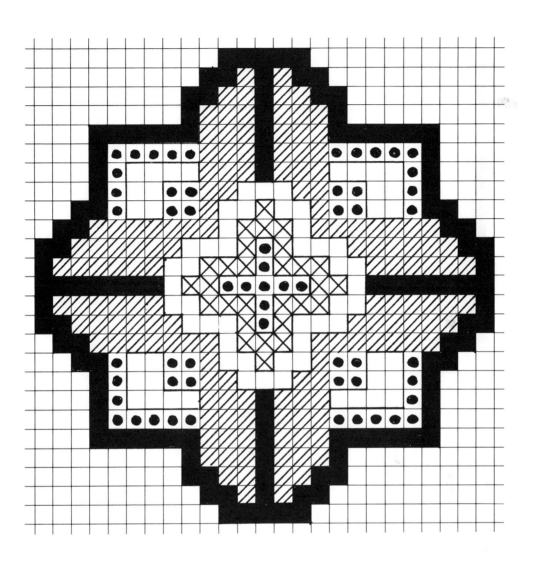

6 7

PERSIAN SCATTER

This charming scatter design is used around the center pattern
in Plate 7 and as a repeat center on page 217. It is commonly
found on rugs from Iran.

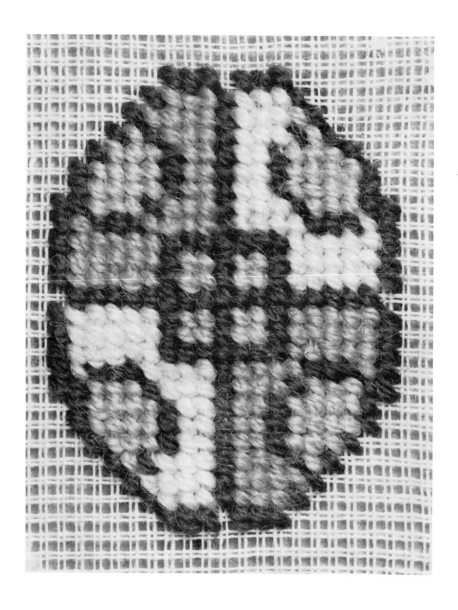

68

RUSSIAN BOKHARA SCATTER

This design comes from a Bokhara rug. Notice that the opposite sides are the same color. This scatter design can easily be enlarged and also used for a center. See pillow in Plate 11, where design is repeated for a center fill-in.

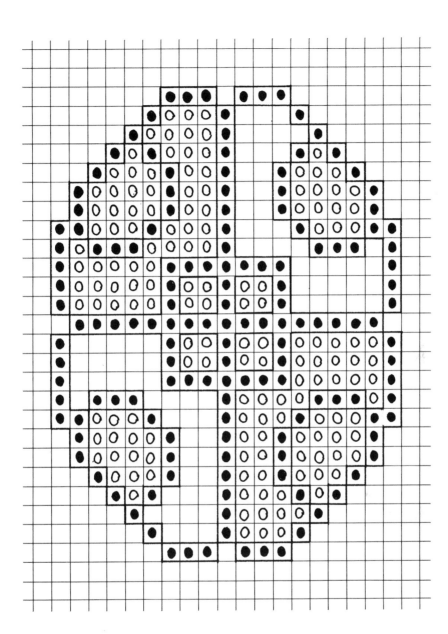

69

TURKISH SCATTER

Found on a Turkish rug, this design is easily enlarged for a rug center. As is, it can be a scatter design or a center. Graph shows slightly more than half of the pattern.

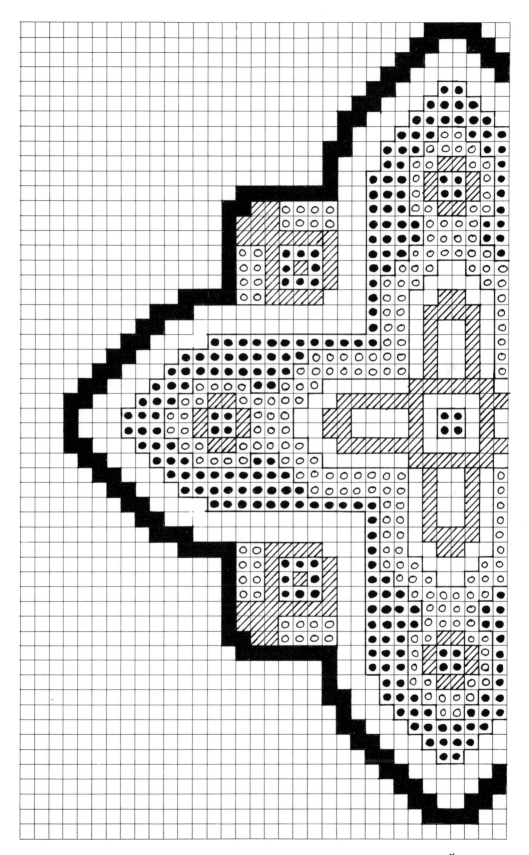

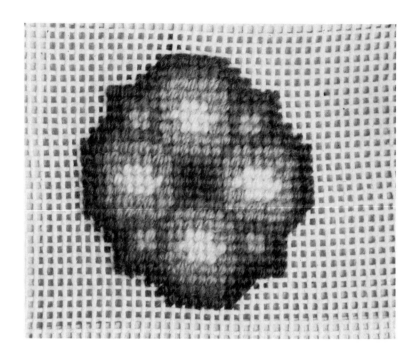

7 o

TURKISH SCATTER

Taken from an antique Turkish rug, this versatile design can
be used as a scatter, a repeat, or enlarged for a center.

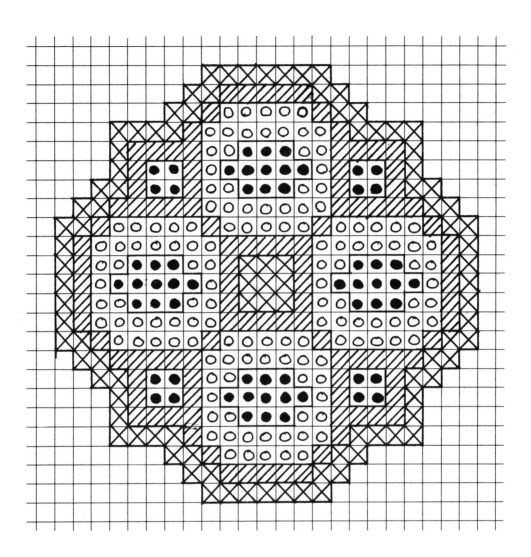

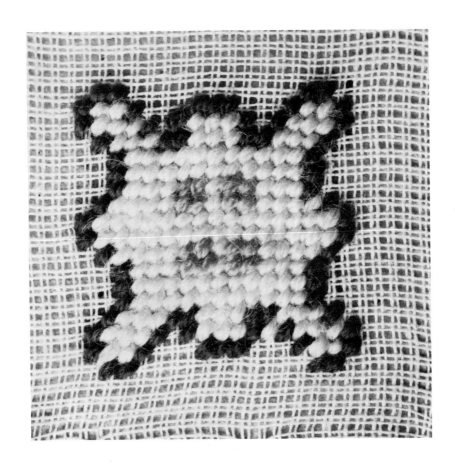

7 [1]

Yugoslavian Scatter

Found on Yugoslavian embroidery, this small scatter design can be used as a repeat pattern or enlarged for a center.

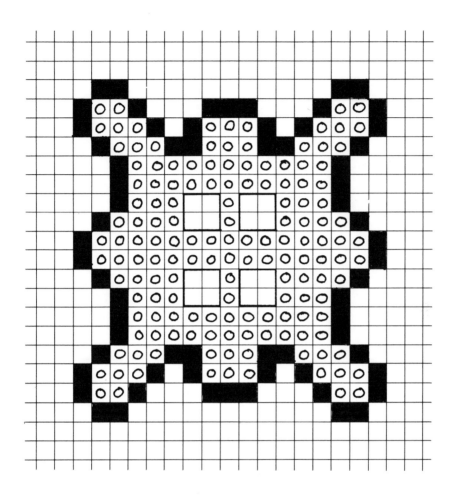

72

YUGOSLAVIAN SCATTER

A Yugoslavian scatter design found on woven fabric, worked in three colors.

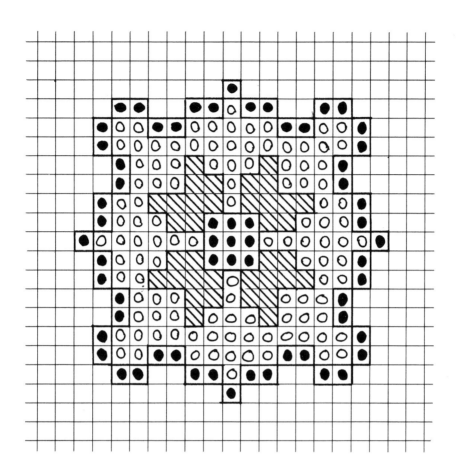

73

 AFGHANISTAN CENTER

A traditional Afghanistan rug design that can be used as a
pillow center or doubled for a rug center. Notice that opposite
sides are the same color. This design consists of thirty-six rows by
forty five rows.

181

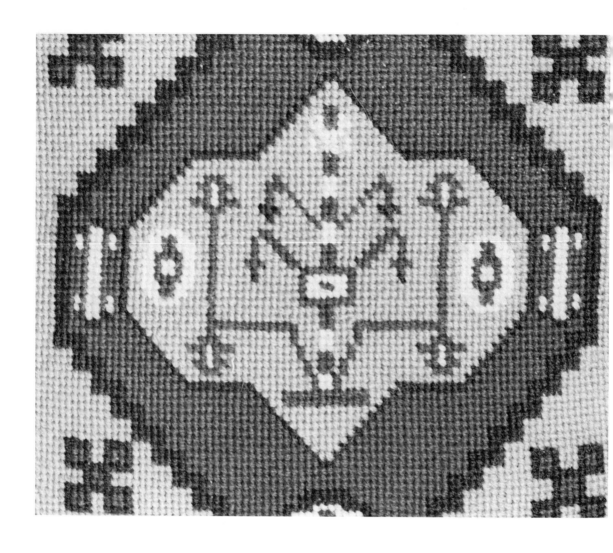

74

Caucasian Center

A delicate center adapted from a nineteenth century Soumak (Caucasian) carpet. Graph shows slightly more than one-half of the pattern.

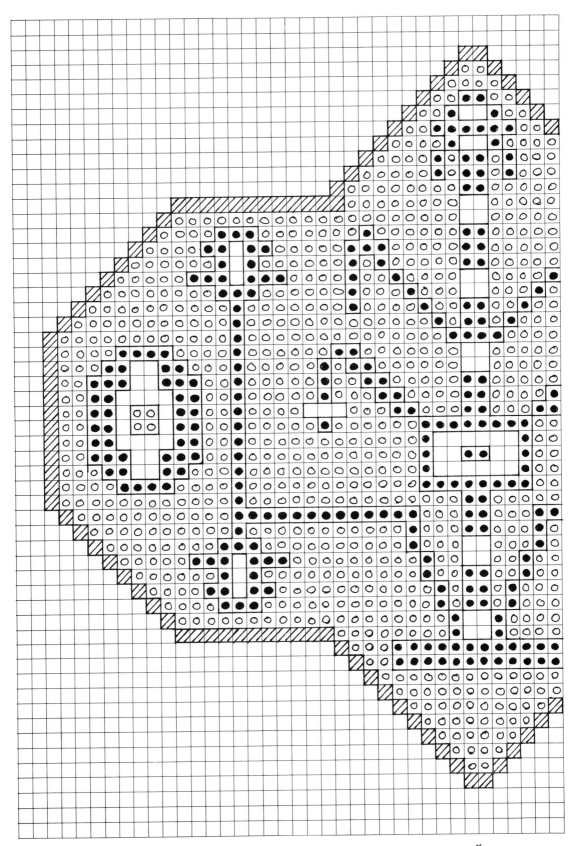

75

Chinese Center

An interesting center adapted from an antique Chinese cushion rug. Note the use of the fret design in the corners. The swastika, originally a symbol of good luck, is frequently shown in much of the early Chinese work.

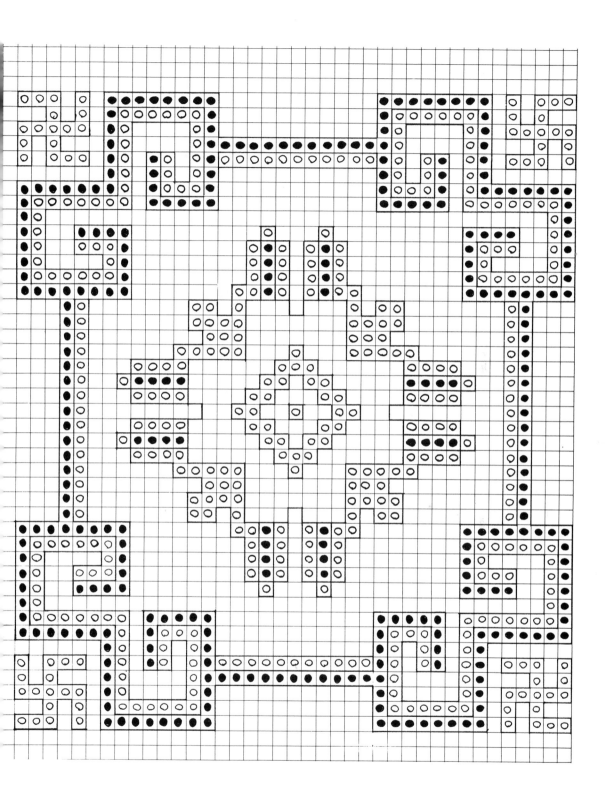

185

76

Dutch Center

An interesting asymmetrical pattern adapted from a Dutch
cross-stitch design. Enlarged to double its size, it makes a nice
center for a pillow.

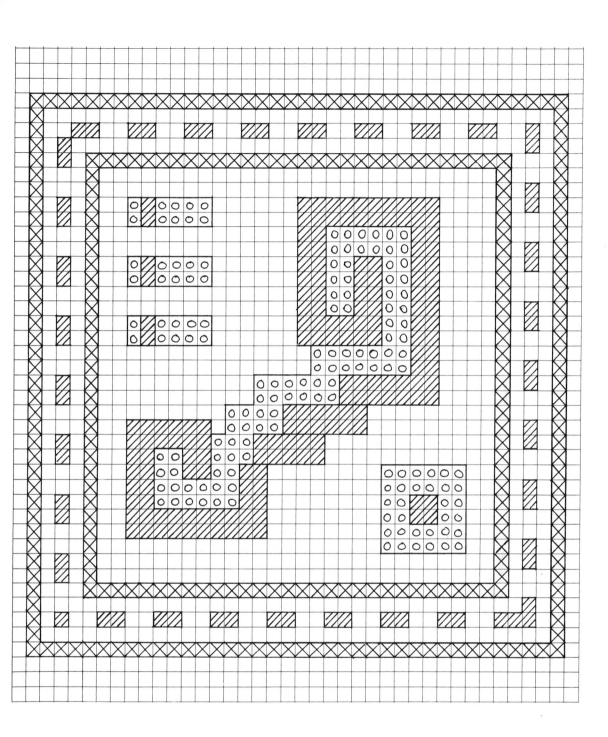

187

77

GREEK CENTER

From Greece, a fascinating design for a pillow center or enlarged
for a rug center. Be sure that each square is outlined in a
different color. Graph shows slightly more than one-quarter of
the design.

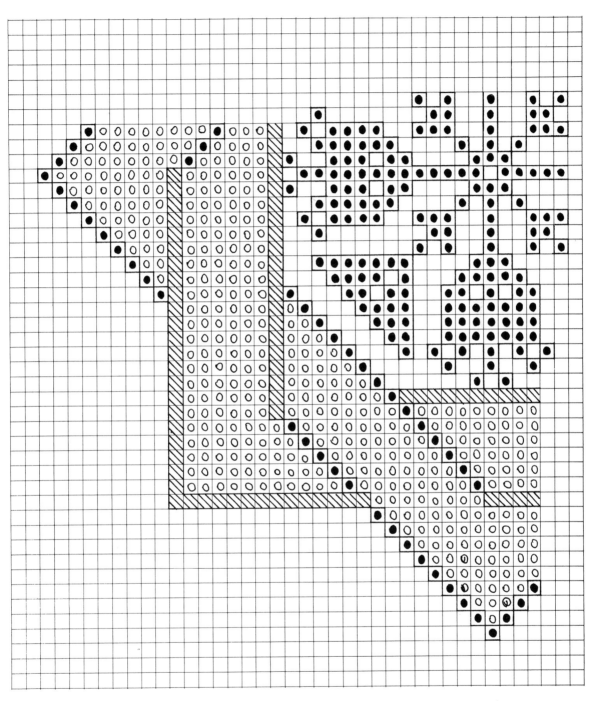

CENTER

189

7 8

GREEK CENTER

Typically Greek, this center design is shown in two colors. You
may decide to do each flower in a different color.

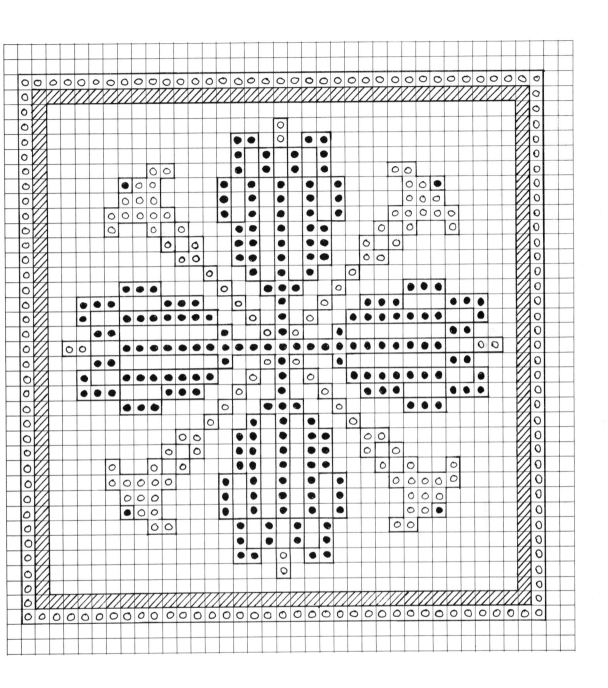

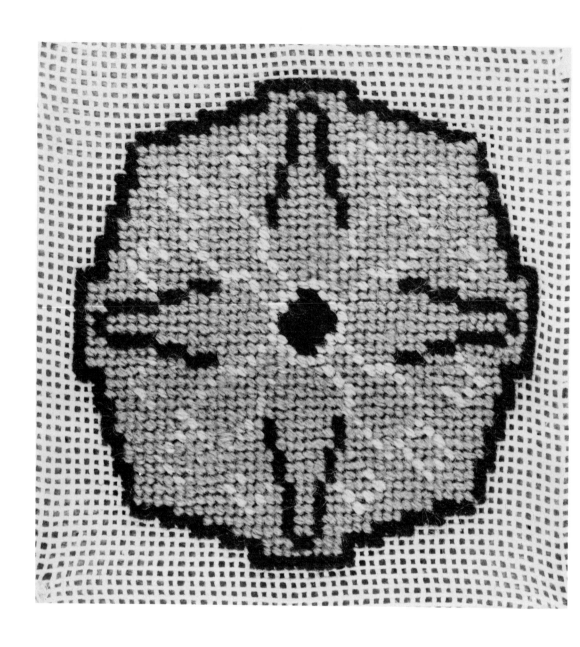

79

JAPANESE CENTER

This feathery Japanese center has been adapted from a
nineteenth-century blue and white porcelain bowl. It is shown
as a forty-six by forty-six stitch design, but by lengthening the
arms or spokes from the center and expanding the outer single
line border, it can be increased considerably with no loss to the
original feeling.

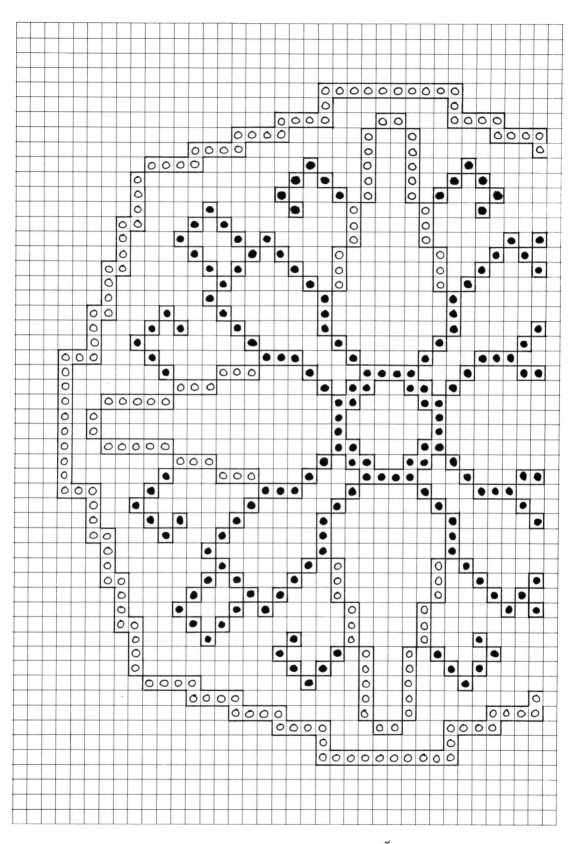

8 o

MEXICAN CENTER

Very Indian in feeling, this design was found on an ancient
Mexican woven fabric. See Plate 13 for pillow with this center.
This sample consists of two colors, but you can vary the design by
adding colors to the corner patterns or changing the center color.

195

8 1

Norwegian Center

From Norway, this design is always done in three colors as shown.
A beautiful center for a pillow or rug. Graph shows exactly
one-quarter of the design.

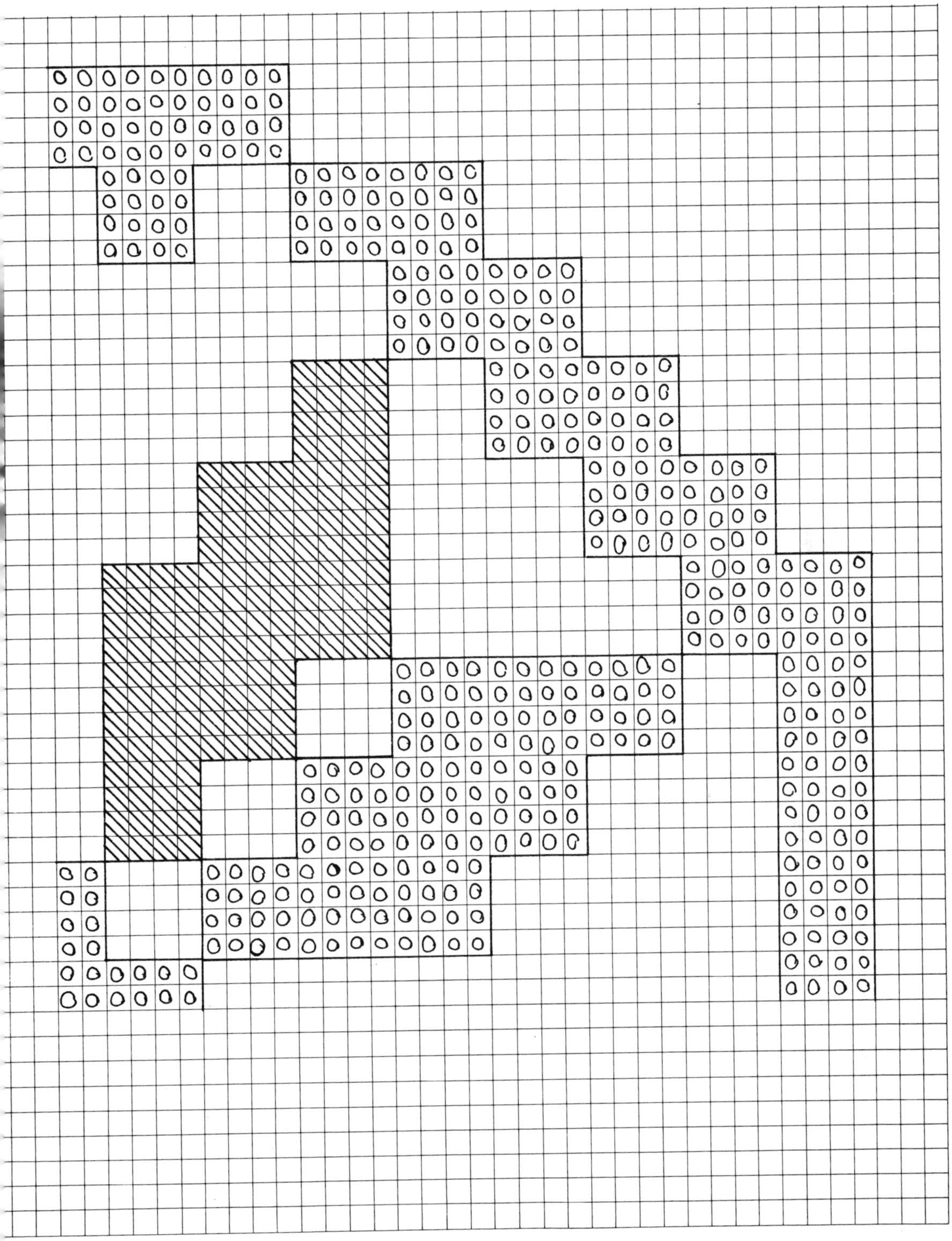

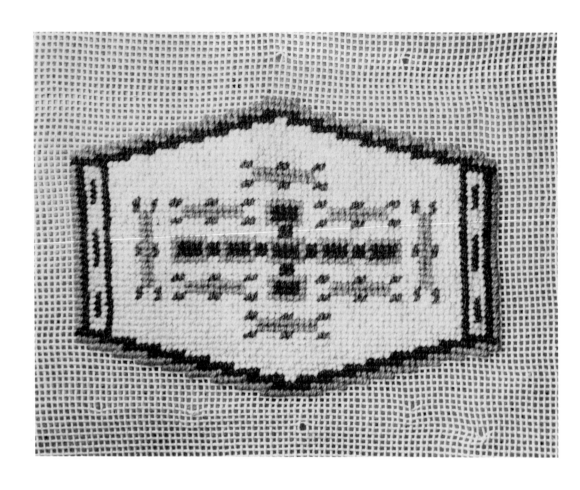

8 2

ORIENTAL CENTER

Of Oriental origin, this center design has much of the feeling
found in American Indian patterns. For a pillow center, follow
graph stitch for stitch. For a rug center, triple or quadruple the
stitches.

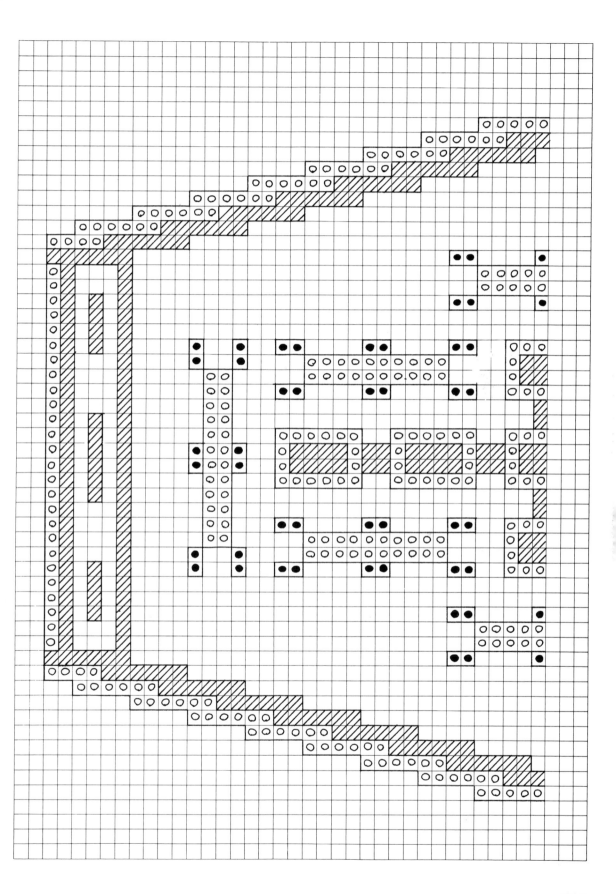

199

8 3

PERSIAN CENTER

An interesting center adapted from a Persian rug. It can be used
on a pillow or enlarged for a rug center. Graph shows
one-quarter of the design.

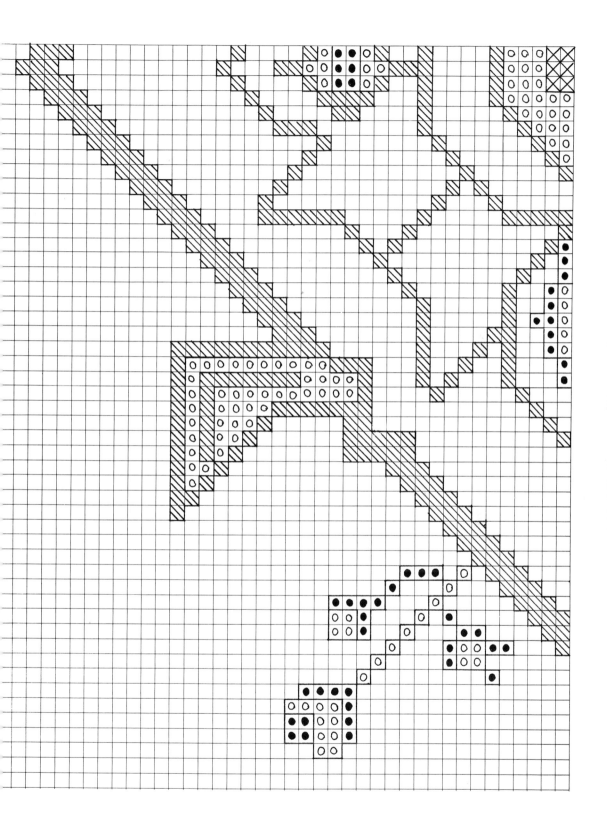

84

Sioux Indian Center

This Sioux Indian star design may be used as a scatter design
without the treelike additions. Graph shows only one of four
trees. With four trees design makes an excellent center. See color
variation of Sioux Indian star in graph samples on page 203.

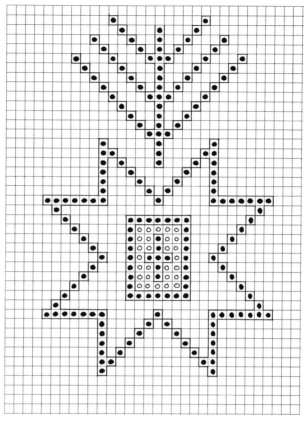

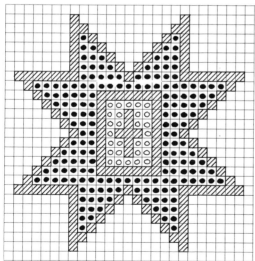

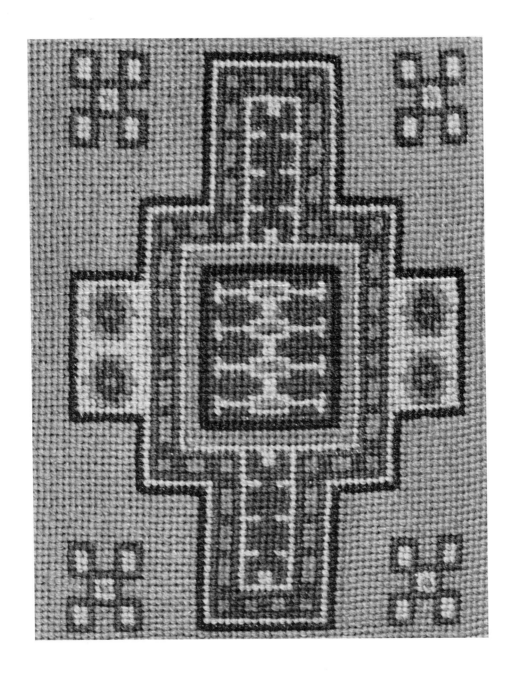

85

TURKISH CENTER

A beautiful center design adapted from a rug of Turkish origin.
Graph shows slightly more than one-quarter of full design.
Needlepoint sample shows pattern with scatter design found on
page 168. For a rug center, double the size.

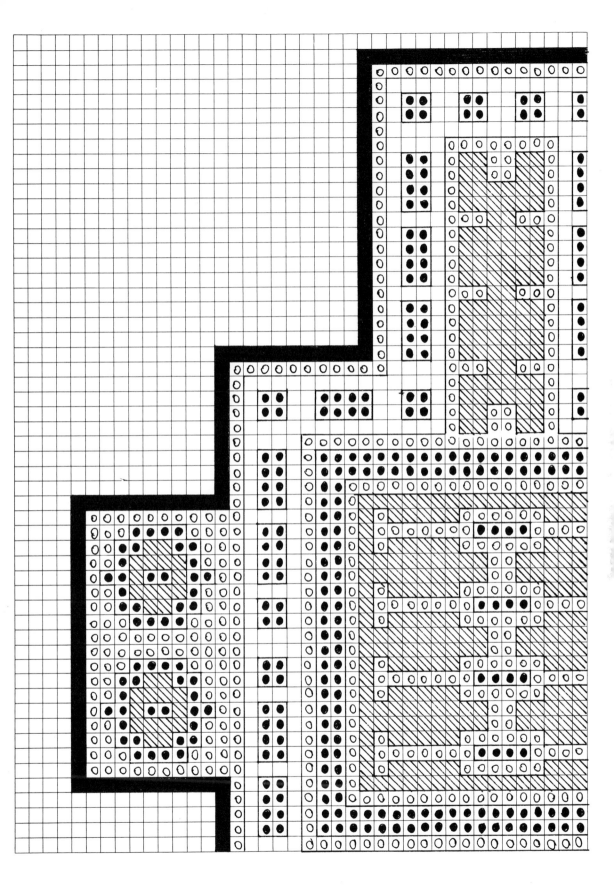

86

Yugoslavian Center

Yugoslavian embroidery inspired this design. Graph shows slightly more than half of the design. Piano bench in Plate 18 uses this pattern done on #14 canvas.

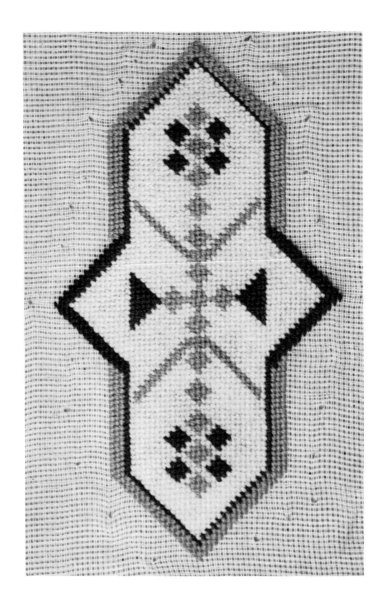

87

ZANZIBAR CENTER

A center design from an African prayer mat found in Zanzibar.
See page 217. Graph shows slightly more than one-quarter of
the design.

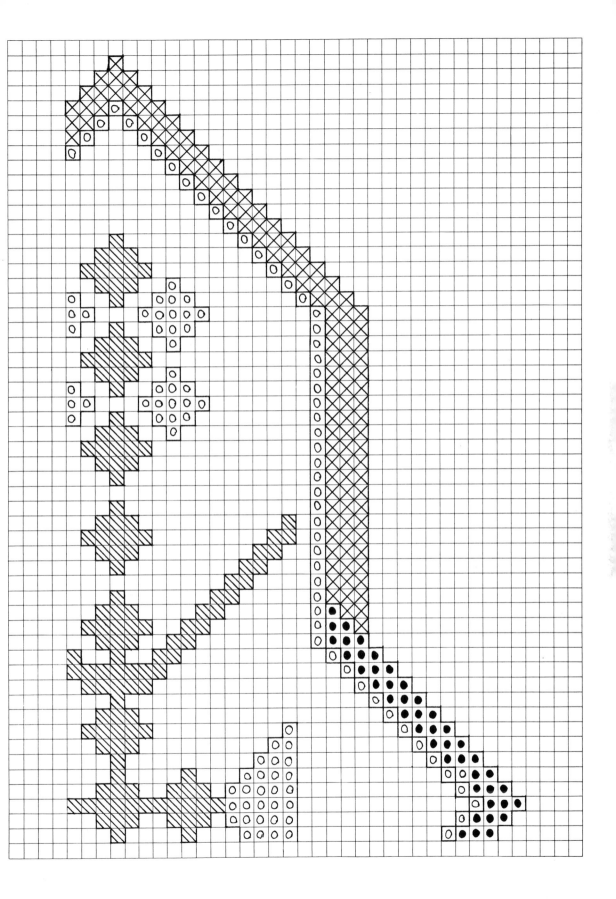

PART VI.

Finished Products

PLATE 1
Oriental rug designs in
striking combination

PLATE 2
African borders and a Greek
center make an attractive
union.

PLATE 3
Designs of Dutch origin done
in a square patchwork type
pillow

PLATE 4
An interesting combination
of a center and borders, all
from Oriental rug designs

PLATE 5
A Caucasian center and
repeated scatter combined
with Persian borders

PLATE 6
Mexican and American
Indian designs were combined
on this rectangular pillow.

PLATE 7
A Turkish center dominates
this bold pillow.

PLATE 8
Multi ethnic designs combined
in small squares

PLATE 9
Barber-pole diagonal stripes
from Afghanistan combined
with a scatter design make an
attractive pillow almost
modern in feeling.

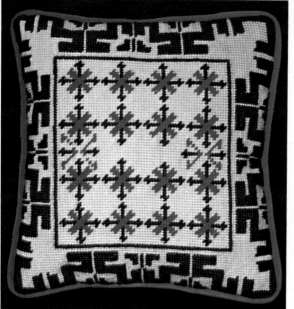

PLATE 10
The border and repeated
scatter designs are all designs
of Greek origin.

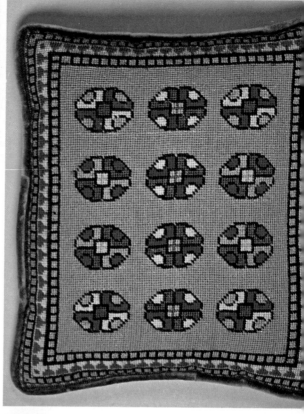

PLATE 11
Here an Oriental scatter
design is repeated in different
color combinations for the
center. Four narrow borders
were used around the edges

PLATE 12
American Indian borders
worked in bands across the
canvas

PLATE 13
All antique Mexican designs
worked in orange, greens,
and black

PLATE 14
Potpourri of pillows

PLATE 15
Caucasian rug design used
on a footstool cover

PLATE 16
These beautifully simple belts
required only two border
designs each. The center belt
is of Norwegian origin. The
two others are from Oriental
rug designs.

PLATE 18
A Yugoslavian repeat design
done on small mesh canvas
makes an interesting and
durable piano-bench cover.

PLATE 17
American Indian wall
hanging

PLATE 19
An antique footstool
upholstered in needlepoint
combining many Turkish and
Persian borders and an
Afghanistan center design

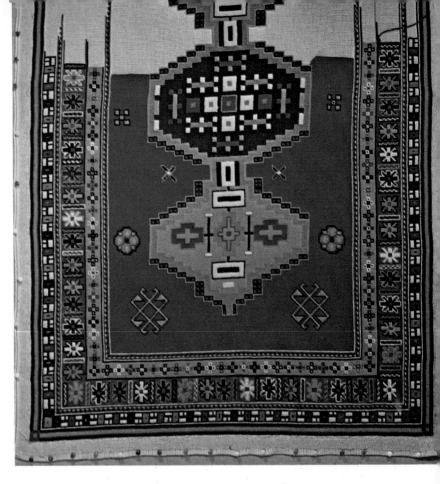

PLATE 20
This rug is worked with five borders, four scatters, and two different centers. Its size is three feet by four-and-a-half feet. All the designs are from Oriental rugs.

PLATE 21
African and Mexican designs combined with narrow Oriental borders make an attractive combination for this rug.

Exclusively Greek designs are combined delicately on this pillow.

A small pillow using Oriental rug designs

American Indian pillow. Notice the effect of the one light–one dark one-row border used twice on this piece.

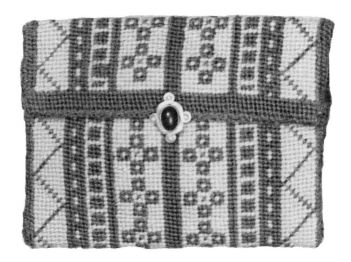

An evening purse worked in two colors using four borders twice each

Bands of borders worked straight across pillow for a pleasant change. Main band is of Norwegian origin.

Oriental rug designs worked mostly in pastel colors

A small Oriental repeated scatter with bold Turkish borders
makes this interesting combination.

An African center dominates this bold combination of designs.

217

Greek, Norwegian, and American Indian designs are combined here smoothly.

A belt worked in two colors using a simple Japanese border design

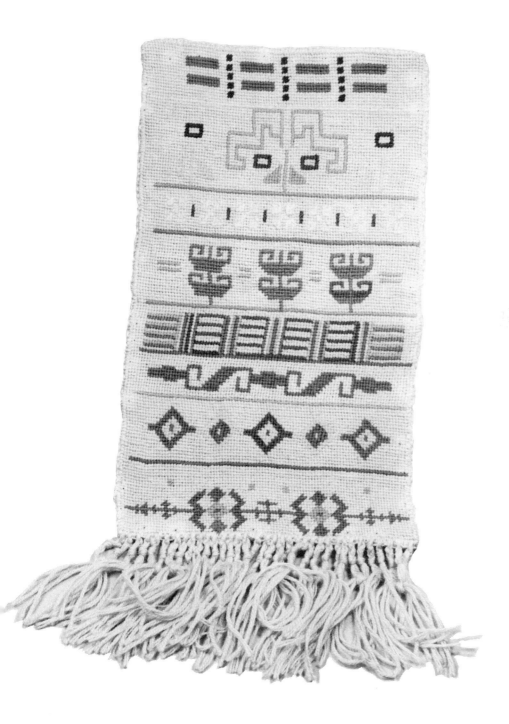

A wall hanging combining border designs of varied origins

Contempory Dutch scatter design surrounded by a field of simple squares

A decorative hanging worked with American Indian, Oriental, and African designs

Greek checkerboard
pattern bordered by
Oriental rug designs

Chinese cushion rug inspired this center design. Border is also
Chinese, originally found on a bowl.

A pillow worked in two colors combines a Japanese center and a Chinese border.

Bold borders of Persian and African origin are used on this small pillow.

222

A many-bordered
pillow of designs
adapted from
Oriental rugs.

This rectangular pillow is worked with two border designs, a
Chinese fret, and a Japanese stencil. The center used a repeated
Chinese scatter design.

Bibliography

Arneberg, Halfdan, *Norwegian Peasant Art, Women's Handicrafts*. Norway, Fabritus and Sonner, 1949.

Beautement, Margaret, *Patterns from Peasant Embroidery*. London, England, B. T. Batsford Limited, 1968.

Bossert, Helmuth, *Decorative Art of Asia and Egypt*. New York, Frederick Praeger, 1956.

Bossert, Helmuth, *Ornaments der Volkunst*. Tubingen, Germany, Verlag Ernst Wasmuth, 1949.

Calatchi, Robert, *Oriental Carpets*. Vermont, Charles E. Tuttle, 1967.

Campana, Michele, *Oriental Carpets*. London, Hamlyn Publishing Ltd., 1969.

Gans-Ruedin, Erwin, *Oriental Carpets*. Bern, Switzerland, Hallwag, 1965.

Hopf, Albrecht, *Oriental Carpets and Rugs*, New York, Viking Press, 1962.

Lewis, G. Griffin, *The Practical Book of Oriental Rugs*. Philadephia & London, J. B. Lippincott Company, 1920.

Liebetrau, Preben, *Oriental Rugs in Color*. New York, Macmillan Company, 1962.

Lyford, Carrie, *Ojbwa (Chippewa) Crafts*. Kansas, Bureau of Indian Affairs, U.S. Department of Interior, 1940.

Lyford, Carrie, *Quill and Beadwork of the Western Sioux*. Kansas, Bureau of Indian Affairs, U.S. Department of Interior, 1943.

Paul, Frances, *Spruce Root Basketry of the Alaskan Tlingit*. Kansas, Bureau of Indian Affairs, U.S. Department of Interior, 1954.

Petrie, William, *Decorative Patterns of the Ancient World*. London, England, W. W. Sprague and Company, 1930.

Index